WITHDRAWN

W9-ACA-310

TWAYNE'S WORLD AUTHORS SERIES

A Survey of the World's Literature

Sylvia E. Bowman, Indiana University

GENERAL EDITOR

AUSTRIA

Ulrich Weisstein, Indiana University

EDITOR

Ferdinand Raimund

(*TWAS* 39)

TWAYNE'S WORLD AUTHORS SERIES (TWAS)

*The purpose of TWAS is to survey the major writers
—novelists, dramatists, historians, poets, philosophers,
and critics—of the nations of the world. Among the
national literatures covered are those of Australia,
Canada, China, Eastern Europe, France, Germany,
Greece, India, Italy, Japan, Latin America, New Zea-
land, Poland, Russia, Scandinavia, Spain, and the
African nations, as well as Hebrew, Yiddish, and
Latin Classical literatures. This survey is comple-
mented by Twayne's United States Authors Series
and English Authors Series.*

*The intent of each volume in these series is to present
a critical-analytical study of the works of the writer;
to include biographical and historical material that
may be necessary for understanding, appreciation,
and critical appraisal of the writer; and to present all
material in clear, concise English—but not to vitiate
the scholarly content of the work by doing so.*

Ferdinand Raimund

By JOHN MICHALSKI

University of Hawaii

Twayne Publishers, Inc.   ::   New York

SALEM COLLEGE LIBRARY
WINSTON-SALEM, N. C.

832.69
R 133
ZM

Copyright © 1968 by Twayne Publishers, Inc.
All Rights Reserved

Library of Congress Catalog Card Number: 67-25203

MANUFACTURED IN THE UNITED STATES OF AMERICA

DEDICATED
to the *Raimundgesellschaft* and the many readers who have been entertained and inspired by the work of Ferdinand Raimund.

"Da streiten sich die Leut herum
Oft um den Wert des Glücks,
Der eine heisst den andern dumm,
Am End weiss keiner nix.
Das ist der allerärmste Mann,
Der andre viel zu reich,
Das Schicksal setzt den Hobel an
Und hobelt s' beide gleich . . ."
Der Verschwender (III, 6)

8 1 4 9 7

Preface

Intended for the general reader as well as for the scholar, this is the first book-length study in English of Ferdinand Raimund's work. It draws upon critical evaluations from both sides of the Atlantic. Since there exists no complete, up-to-date bibliography on Raimund, every effort was taken to render the Selected Bibliography at the end of this book as useful as possible. Raimund scholarship began as a set of anecdotes and impressions in the playwright's own life-time until literary scholars began to scrutinize his work. References to Raimund's plays in this study are based on Friedrich Schreyvogl's edition (Munich: Winkler Verlag, 1960), which follows the text of the definitive edition by Fritz Brukner and Eduard Castle, now out-of-print and generally unavailable.

Raimund is considered the leading playwright of the Old Viennese Popular Theater tradition. The Old Viennese Popular Theater, in turn, constitutes Austria's significant gift to European drama of the Nineteenth Century. The origins of this tradition are to be found in the major European theater movements that preceded it: German and Austrian Folk Theater, *Commedia dell'Arte*, the Jesuit Theater, Baroque Court Opera, and the English and German travelling theater companies.

Like Shakespeare and Molière before him, Raimund was both actor and playwright. A master of the comic farce, he will be remembered for his eight notable plays, which are analyzed in this study. Both his life and his work gave rise to the Raimund legend, that manifested itself in poetry as well as in plays and novels. Raimund's strength lies in his humorous pathos, which he formulated out of the deep consciousness of his social environment. His works originally stood apart from the classical tradition of the *Burgtheater*. This distinction was erased when Austria's literary critics elevated Raimund's plays to classical status and they were performed at the *Burgtheater*. In the twentieth century, some of his plays were also made into movies. Admirers and scholars founded the *Raimundgesellschaft*, and there exists a literary prize named after him.

Well known in Europe, Raimund has been available in English primarily through Erwin Tramer's recent translation of *Der Verschwender*. Hopefully, Professor Corliss Edwin Phillabaum, who translated *Der Bauer als Millionär* and *Der Alpenkönig und der Menschenfeind* as part of his doctoral thesis, will make these translations available to the English reader.

My initial acquaintance with Raimund's plays dates from pre-World War II days in Vienna. Since then I have occasionally returned to his magic world to nurture a nostalgia for a poetic era that probably will not be duplicated again. It was thus with pleasure and satisfaction that I accepted to undertake this project. If it succeeds in providing a current and objective evaluation of the career and work of Raimund, it will have achieved its purpose.

HONOLULU, HAWAII   JOHN MICHALSKI

Acknowledgments

There are many people to whom I owe gratitude for their good wishes, assistance, and helpful advice in completing this project. For the initial setting up of my bibliography, I am indebted to Dr. Hans Pauer, Director of Picture Archives at the Austrian National Library. For a final check of this bibliography, thanks are due to Professor Margaret Dietrich of the Institute for Theater Research at the University of Vienna. Dr. Christl Pernold of the Austrian National Library kindly supplied me with microfilms containing out-of-print material. I am also indebted to the staff of the University of Hawaii Sinclair Library, particularly to Dean Ralph R. Shaw, Mrs. Clarissa H. Halsted, Miss Emily O. Garnett, Miss Genevieve B. Correa, and many others.

For advice, reprints of their articles, and encouragement, I am indebted to Professor Heinz Politzer, University of California at Berkeley, Professor O. Paul Straubinger, University of California at Riverside, and Professor emeritus Arthur Burkhard of Harvard University. For further helpful assistance I am thankful to Garth McCann of Ohio State University. I am also grateful to the University of Hawaii Research Council for a grant to defray some of the costs of my research material. Invaluable was the aid rendered by Dr. Gustav Pichler, President of the *Raimundgesellschaft*. Thanks are also due to Dr. Edith Heinze, daughter of Dr. Otto Rommel, who answered my communications to her ailing father. To Professor Ulrich Weisstein of Indiana University I am indebted for a number of technical pointers in this venture.

Acknowledgment is due to Professor Corliss Edwin Phillabaum of the University of Wisconsin at Milwaukee for permission to quote excerpts from his unpublished English translations of Raimund's *Der Bauer als Millionär* and *Der Alpenkönig und der Menschenfeind*. For permission to reprint excerpts from Erwin

Tramer's translation of *Der Verschwender*, I am indebted to Mr. Frederick Ungar of the Frederick Ungar Publishing Co., New York. Raimund's photograph was acquired through the services of the Picture Archives of the Austrian National Library.

Contents

Chronology

1776   Establishment of the *Burgtheater* in Vienna.

1781   The *Leopoldstädter Theater* opens its doors under Karl Marinelli. It is later renamed the *Carl Theater*.

1787   *Theater an der Wieden,* after 1801 known as the *Theater an der Wien,* opens.

1788   The *Josefstädter Theater* is established under Karl Mayer.

1790   June 1, Ferdinand is born as the son of Jakob and Katharina Reimann (also spelled: Reymann, Reymund, and Raymond) at 45 Mariahilfer Strasse in suburban Vienna. As an actor, Ferdinand changes his name to Raimund.

1800   Raimund attends St. Anne's Elementary School, where he excels in French and in playing the violin.

1802   March 26, his mother (1753–1802) dies of a pulmonary disease.

1804   November 29, his father (1745–1804) also dies of pulmonary complications. Raimund moves in with his older sister Anna and her husband.

1805–   Earns his first money as a bakery apprentice and seller of
1808   candy and liquid refreshments at the *Josefstädter Theater* and the *Burgtheater*.

1808–   Gives up his job at the bakery and takes on his first acting
1814   roles with travelling companies of players at Meidling, Pressburg, Ödenburg, Steinamanger, and Raab.

1814   The Congress of Vienna convenes. Playwright-director Alois Gleich gives Raimund his first important acting role at the *Josefstädter Theater:* In April he appears as Feldkümmel in August Kotzebue's *Pächter Feldkümmels Hochzeitstag;* in May as Franz Moor in Friedrich Schiller's *Die Räuber.* Raimund slavishly imitates the mannerisms of the actor Ferdinand Ochsenheimer.

SALEM COLLEGE LIBRARY
WINSTON-SALEM, N. C.

1815   March 28, he becomes popular as an actor in the role of Kratzerl in Alois Gleich's *Musikanten auf dem Hohenmarkt*. In August he makes guest appearances at the *Leopoldstädter Theater*.

1816   Raimund tries his hand at directing at the *Josefstädter Theater*. Makes guest appearances at the *Leopoldstädter Theater* and the *Hietzing Theater*.

1817   Makes guest appearances at the *Theater an der Wien*, also at the theaters in Baden and Hietzing. In October Raimund joins the *Leopoldstädter Theater*, where he appears in Gleich's *Weissvogels Witwerstand* under the direction of Leopold Huber.

1818   Raimund has a love affair with Therese Grünthal. When he encounters this fickle girl in the company of another man, he gives her a public thrashing, is arrested for assault and battery, and serves a commuted sentence of three days in jail. Dissatisfied with the text of certain plays in which he appears, Raimund inserts his own humorous passages to make them more palatable. Between July and September he makes guest appearances at the *Baden Theater*.

1819   Raimund falls in love with Toni Wagner, the attractive daughter of a coffee house owner. When Toni's parents refuse to allow her to marry him, he has a nervous breakdown. He is nursed back to health by the actress Luise Gleich. He makes guest appearances at the *Baden Theater*.

1820   April 2, shotgun wedding of Luise Gleich and Ferdinand. Ferdinand, however, does not show up for the ceremony. The wedding finally takes place on April 8. The marriage is beset by endless quarrels, nagging, and unfaithfulness. On October 7, his wife gives birth to a girl, Amalia, who dies a few weeks later.

1821   Raimund signs a long-term contract with the *Leopoldstädter Theater*. Husband and wife separate. In September Raimund goes back to Toni Wagner. Since he cannot legally remarry, a private ceremony is performed near Neustift on September 10.

1822   Luise divorces Ferdinand on January 22.

1823   In August Raimund makes guest appearances at the *Baden Theater* and performs for Austrian Emperor Francis II.

Friends encourage him to write a play of his own. When Carl Meisl does not come through with an assigned play, Raimund writes it himself in October and November. December 18, his first play, *Der Barometermacher auf der Zauberinsel* (*Barometermaker on the Magic Isle*), premieres at the *Leopoldstädter Theater*. Raimund plays the title role. The play is a great success.

1824   During the summer, Raimund makes guest appearances at the *Baden Theater*. December 17, his second play, *Der Diamant des Geisterkönigs* (*The Diamond of the Spirit King*), opens at the *Leopoldstädter Theater* and is equally successful. Raimund appears in the role of Florian Waschblau.

1825   Real and imagined illnesses plague Raimund as he abandons the stage between May and September. To recuperate he takes trips to Linz, Mariazell, and Bad Ischl. Friends present him with a commemorative medal when he resumes his work at the theater.

1826   On June 13, his sister Anna dies. Raimund joins a group of actors, painters, and writers at the "Silbernes Kaffeehaus." During the summer he takes a journey to Salzburg. November 10, Raimund's third play, *Das Mädchen aus der Feenwelt oder Der Bauer als Millionär* (*The Maiden from the Fairy World or The Peasant as Millionaire*), opens at the *Leopoldstädter Theater*. Raimund plays Fortunatus Wurzel and Therese Krones, Jugend.

1827   *Der Diamant des Geisterkönigs* is given at Prague under the direction of J. A. Stöger. September 25, Raimund's *Moisasurs Zauberfluch* (*Moisasur's Magic Curse*) is staged at the *Theater an der Wien*. The audiences are puzzled by his attempts to raise the level of the Old Viennese Popular Theater.

1828   January 8, Raimund's fifth play, *Die gefesselte Phantasie* (*The Inhibited Imagination*) performed at the *Leopoldstädter Theater*. Raimund plays harpist Nachtigall. The play is only moderately successful. On April 3, Raimund becomes artistic director at the *Leopoldstädter Theater*, a position he holds until August 1, 1830. On October 17, his next play, *Der Alpenkönig und der Menschenfeind* (*Moun-*

tain King and Misanthrope), opens at the *Leopoldstädter Theater*. Raimund plays the misanthrope Rappelkopf.

1829   On December 4, Raimund's seventh play, *Die unheilbringende Krone* (*The Fatal Crown*), premiered at the *Leopoldstädter Theater* and was poorly received. It inspired the parody *Goldpapierne Zauberkrone oder Nichts ist unmöglich* (*The Goldpaper Magic Crown or Nothing is Impossible*).

1830   In August, Raimund leaves the *Leopoldstädter Theater*, intending to accept only guest appearances. In the autumn, he appears at the *Theater an der Wien*, primarily in his own plays.

1831   January 24, the English comedian John Baldwin Buckstone produces an English rendition of *Der Alpenkönig und der Menschenfeind* at the Adelphi Theater in London. During the summer, Raimund takes trips to Gutenstein and other parts of Austria and Bavaria. He makes guest appearances at various Austrian and German theaters.

1832   Between April and June Raimund performs at the *Königsstädtisches Theater* in Berlin. He is so successful that the management offers him the directorship of this theater, which he turns down. In September and October, he appears in Hamburg.

1833   Raimund makes guest appearances at the *Josefstädter Theater* between January and April, and during November and December. He works on his next play. Takes occasional trips to various parts of Austria.

1834   On February 20, Raimund's eighth play, *Der Verschwender* (*The Spendthrift*) is given at the *Josefstädter Theater*. He plays the loyal servant Valentin. This play, his last, is his most popular one both during his lifetime and afterwards. In September he buys a house in Gutenstein, where he lives with his common-law wife Toni until his death. In the autumn and the following spring he makes guest appearances at various theaters.

1836   During February and March Raimund appears as Wurzel, Valentin, Florian, and Rappelkopf in Prague. In April and May he performs at the *Hamburg Stadttheater*, where he gives his last acting performance. In August he is bitten by a dog and imagines himself infected with rabies. On August 29, he and Toni set out for Vienna to consult a physician. A severe storm forces them to stay overnight at the inn "Zum Hirschen" in Pottenstein. After a sleepless night, he attempts to commit suicide. He dies on September 5, after some of Vienna's top surgeons have vainly tried to save his life. On September 8, he is buried at Gutenstein. On September 17, Mozart's *Requiem* is performed at the Church in Leopoldstadt to commemorate his death. On October 22, Carl Meisl's one-act play, *Ein Blümchen auf Raimunds Grab* (*A Flower on Raimund's Grave*), is given at the *Josefstädter Theater.*

1837 On September 8, Raimund's tomb is unveiled and blessed at the cemetery in Gutenstein. The German Theater in Pest organizes a Raimund Celebration, in which the actor Johann Lang appears as Raimund.

1849 Raimund's *Der Diamant des Geisterkönigs* is adapted for the Danish stage by Hans Christian Andersen.

1855 Luise Gleich-Raimund dies.

1879 Toni Wagner, Raimund's common-law wife, dies completely impoverished.

1885 June 18, Raimund's *Der Verschwender* is his first play to be given at the venerable *Burgtheater.* Rudolf Tyrolt appears as the servant Valentin.

1886 Friends unveil a commemorative plaque at Pottenstein.

1893 The *Wiener Spielhaus* becomes the *Raimund Theater,* which today is the home of the operetta in Vienna.

1898 Vogl's Raimund monument is unveiled in May near the *Volkstheater.* Johann Strauss plays "Klänge aus der Raimundzeit," Op. 99.

1935 Establishment of the *Raimundgesellschaft.*

1940 The city of Vienna puts on a Raimund Celebration between June 1–9.

1957 The Raimund Museum in Gaaden is opened to the public.

1961 On October 23, the Raimund Hall in the Austrian Cultural Center, Palais Palffy, is opened to the public.

CHAPTER 1

The Old Viennese Popular Theater

THE Old Viennese Popular Theater, known in German as *Alt-Wiener Volkskomödie* or *Alt-Wiener Volkstheater,* should not be confused with the *Volksschauspiel* or folk play, which preceded it, influenced it, and flourished alongside it. The *Volksschauspiel* tradition[1] has its origins in early history and differs from the Old Viennese Popular Theater in that it is not professional, and in that its authors and adaptors are generally anonymous.

The *Volksschauspiel* flourished largely in Alpine regions and other comparatively secluded areas of Austria and Germany. Its chief forms are the *Passionsspiel* (*Passion Play*), the *Weihnachtsspiel* (*Christmas Play*), the *Legendenspiel* (*Legend Play*), and the *Puppenspiel* (*Puppet Play*). These folk plays were performed during Christmas, the Carnival Season, and at various local and religious holidays. Folk plays have a minimum of plot and tend to incorporate fresh material each year. Actors in the folk theater are amateurs who band together in associations along professional lines. They have no permanent stages. Stage plays from the classical repertoire are sometimes adapted to the folk theater tradition, resulting in simplified, popularized versions of the originals. The Austrian folk theater continues to thrive to this day in the provinces of Styria, Carinthia, and Burgenland. The puppet play has been most popular in the metropolitan centers and has received its maximum development in Vienna.

I *Origins*

For centuries, Vienna has been a significant cultural center in Europe. Cultural activities of one type or another have been enhanced by this city's favorable geographical location between East and West, and its emphasis on both tradition and change.

This receptive climate furthered the establishment of a theater movement that was unique to Vienna, and which is now apreciated in other parts of the world, namely the Old Viennese Popular Theater. This novel dramatic form originated in the principal theater movements of Europe during the eighteenth and nineteenth centuries. Seeking to entertain and enlighten, it became an eclectic theater that accepted influences from many sources.

The Austrian folk play has given amateur performers in scattered agrarian and mountain regions an opportunity for artistic expression in a manner most suitable to the locality and the mood of that particular area. This form of theater included features of the comic character Hanswurst, and a variety of approaches to the art of puppetry, turning the folk play into a form of entertainment enjoyed by young and old alike.

Peter Raas, a farmer who became famous for his portrayal of the comic character Hanswurst, is a direct precursor of Anton Stranitzky and Gottfried Prehauser, two playwrights active in the early stages of the Old Viennese Popular Theater tradition.[2] Hanswurst also became a stock character in puppet play performances. One of the better-known puppet Hanswursts, created by Johann Boeckl, has been preserved for posterity and is on view in the Upper Austrian Provincial Museum at Linz.[3] Two of the more popular adaptations of the folk theater from the classical drama were Friedrich Schiller's *Maria Stuart* and *Die Jungfrau von Orleans* (*Maiden of Orleans*).[4]

The *Commedia dell'Arte*, a comedy of masks and improvisations, had its beginnings in sixteenth century Italy, and soon thereafter found its way north to Vienna.[5] Initially the Italian comedians performed at the Imperial Court in Vienna; later they were engaged by the lesser nobility, and eventually catered to the general public. Even though the Italian language was not readily understood by the masses, they could easily follow stylized plots and identify stock characters. These were skeleton plots, filled out with jokes, stories, and acrobatics appropriate to the situation or mood of the locale. The essence of artistry in the *Commedia dell'Arte* was not originality, but rather variations on a well-known theme.

The skeleton plot centered around two young lovers called *innamorati*. Actors came prepared with the following stock devices

[20]

to fill out the action of the play: clever retorts or *battute,* imaginative and spontaneous ideas or *concetti,* to which were later added the eye-filling, ear-shattering intermission acts or *lazzi.* Sometimes shorter intermission spectacles or *burles* were performed. Love was the basic theme, and confusion and conspiracy the motivating forces for the action. At its best, the *Commedia dell'Arte* created an atmosphere in which everyone was conspiring and plotting against everyone else.

Each company of players consisted of a number of stock characters who served to fill out the skeleton plot. The young lovers, aided by ingenious servants, frequently managed to outwit their elders. The *Capitano,* a braggart of the first order, always managed to put his foot in his mouth or foul things up for the lovers. Hundreds of spontaneous variations were played upon the basic theme of the *Commedia.* Invariably there appeared a clown Harlequin or *Arlecchino.* The playwrights Carlo Gozzi (1720–1806) and Carlo Goldoni (1707–1793) contributed towards making the *Commedia dell'Arte* into a literary form that gradually moved away from skeleton plots towards fully developed actions. In Goldoni's more than one hundred plays, stock characters began to give way to individualized human beings, and interesting situations taken from the milieu of his native Venice. Gozzi's plays stayed closer to the original form of the *Commedia dell'Arte.* He was particularly influential in Vienna after his works had been translated by Clemens August Werthes.

The language of the *Commedia dell'Arte,* like that of the early Old Viennese Popular Theater, was customarily the local dialect of a particular area. The complete or skeleton texts were invariably changed to suit specific events and circumstances. From the sixteenth century on, Italian comedians competed with English comedians for the attention of the Austrian populace. And since the theater was a popular entertainment, the nation's populace patronized both.

Another impetus to the Old Viennese Popular Theater was derived from the Jesuit Theater, which had its roots in the Humanistic Renaissance school drama of Wolfgang Schmeltzl (1500–1557), who produced *Das Spiel vom verlorenen Sohn* (The *Play of the Prodigal Son*) in 1540. This theatrical movement culminated in the dramas of Nikolaus Avancinus (1612–1686).

The motto of the Jesuit Theater was "Ad majorem Dei gloriam" ("For God's Greater Glory"). It served as a means for instructing the youth in matters of Catholic faith and dogma. Conveying the Catholic way of life by means of colorful and eye-catching magic plays seemed more rewarding than the arduous road of extended intellectual debates.

The golden era of the Jesuit Theater coincided with that of the Baroque Court Opera. Avancinus' most famous play was *Pietas Victrix (Victorious Piety)*, performed in 1659 in the presence of Emperor Leopold I. The allegorical and fairy-tale elements contained in it were precursors of similar elements in the early products of the Old Viennese Theater. At times the Jesuit plays were performed amidst great pomp and splendor with a cast of several hundred actors. Music, singing, and dancing were integral parts of such performances. Stage effects included the depiction of flying objects, infernal noises, fantastic colors and lights, and surprise appearances of predatory animals. The action took place on a three-level stage. This frank attempt by the Jesuit Theater to reach the largest number of people, in a move to offset the gains of the Reformation, was largely crowned with success.

Of the more than several thousand Jesuit plays performed in Vienna, only a very few were written down. Similar to the *Commedia dell'Arte,* the Jesuit plays commenced with skeleton plots that derived their structure from the Holy Scriptures. These Jesuit plays were later enlarged into magnificent productions that could not leave the general populace wholly disinterested. The transition from the Jesuit Theater to the Old Viennese Popular Theater occurred in the work of the Silesian Johann Baptist Adolph (1657–1708).[6] This transitional process gained momentum with the innovation of enclosures, which were scenes of life in beautiful Vienna, spiced with local jokes and songs.

The opera originated in Venice and Florence and was introduced into Austria, by way of Salzburg, as early as 1618.[7] A short time thereafter, it reached Vienna, where Francesco Cavalli produced his operas *Egisto* and *Giasone*. In order to make operas more exciting and interesting, they were soon enlarged with inserts called *Freudenspiele,* which consisted of ballet performances, songs and folk dancing.[8]

In due time, this operatic import from Italy developed into the

Wiener Prunkoper or Viennese Baroque Opera, a form of extravagant entertainment, staged elaborately and featuring colorful and bizarre costumes. At its height, the Viennese Baroque Opera was unrivalled in Europe. Leopold I celebrated his marriage to Margaretha of Spain in 1666 with the performance of Marco Antonio Cesti's pretentious opera *Il pomo d'oro* (*The Golden Apple*). This opera was performed by several hundred actors and witnessed by thousands of spectators.

Aurelio Amaltheo has been credited with the introduction of Hanswurst and Harlequin into the opera at the beginning of the second half of the seventeenth century.[9] Antonio Draghi was then Vienna's leading court composer and Nicolo Minto the outstanding lyricist. Characteristic features of the Viennese Baroque Opera that paved the way for the early Old Viennese Popular Theater included its stock characters inherited from the *Commedia dell'Arte*, the intermission inserts with Hanswurst, themes derived from classical antiquity and mythology, plots concerned with love and cuckoldry complicated into impossible situations, and an extensive stage machinery. The court poets Apostolo Zeno (1668–1750) and Pietro Metastasio (1698–1782) were instrumental in eliminating comical intrusions, thus initiating a new phase in operatic history.[10]

The Habsburg dynasty tacitly encouraged the development of cultural pursuits by personally participating in them from time to time. Charles IV wrote operatic arias, frequently conducted his court orchestra and encouraged the future Empress Maria Theresia in her singing and dancing. With the passing of Charles IV, some of the pomp and splendor were taken out of the Viennese Baroque Opera. Operatic reforms were initiated by Christoph Willibald Gluck and accomplished in the operas of Wolfgang Amadeus Mozart.

Not only operatic productions were received with enthusiasm by the populace. The English and German travelling theater companies constituted another popular source of entertainment. "Schaffts die Wäsch' fort, die Komödianten kommen!" ("Get the wash down, the comedians are coming!") shouted the women, when a company of wandering players entered a town. English and, later, indigenous German companies of travelling actors constituted an additional source of the Old Viennese Popular Theater. Originally under the protection of rich nobles, the English groups had performed largely in their native country. Eventually they travelled abroad to Holland, Germany, and Austria. Although they carried little or no scenery with them, they did bring along their colorful native costumes. Thus lightly encumbered, they roved at will, ready to amuse the gathering of great noblemen in their castles or a humbler audience in the village. Actor-playwrights wrote to please their discriminating audiences. Of them only those survived who were clever enough to sense the spirit of the time and able to please groundlings and gallants alike. Thomas Kyd, Christopher Marlowe, and others in whose footsteps Shakespeare followed, were among the most popular.

These English comedians enhanced the development of professional acting on the suburban Viennese stage. Some of the original foreign groups stayed on in the country and were integrated into the Austrian theater. Gradually, indigenous Austrian and German companies absorbed these English troupes. The original Elizabethan theater repertory expanded to include also plays by Molière and Goldoni, as well as improvised *Haupt-und Staatsaktionen* or plays about events taking place in the highest social and political circles. By its example the Viennese Baroque Opera encouraged these travelling theater companies to enlarge their scope and produce more elaborate stage productions.

The Folk Play, the *Commedia dell'Arte,* the Jesuit Theater, and the Viennese Baroque Opera supplied technical devices and skills for the presentation of extravaganzas, while the English and German companies of wandering players furnished the needed organizational structure and the actors.

The comparatively strict censorship under which all Viennese theaters operated forced the development of the Old Viennese Popular Theater into a mold of its own. Certain social, political, and religious themes were eliminated from the stage, thus taxing the ingenuity of playwrights to write entertaining and meaningful plays that would appeal to their audiences without antagonizing the zealous censors. While reformers were depriving the Jesuit Theater and the Viennese Baroque Opera of much of its spontaneous humor and buffoonery, the Old Viennese Popular Theater became its repository.

going to live longer than the forever intriguing noblemen. While the masses looked up to the members of the nobility and sometimes even admired them, they rarely wished to exchange their lot for that of their more fortunate brethren.

In his plays Stranitzky not only employed the popular themes of others, but also drew on the music of the Viennese Baroque Opera. The early form of the Old Viennese Popular Theater was that of the *Singspiel* or musical comedy, closely akin to the operetta. In these musical comedies Stranitzky ridiculed the extravagances and impossible situations of the Viennese Baroque Opera. It was this type of playful and amiable parody by one artistic form of another that produced an atmosphere receptive to a great variety of dramatic experiments. The forever-present Hanswurst personified the average man's reactions to his existential limitations. Hanswurst's purpose in the theater has been likened to that of the Greek chorus.[11] He represented the uninhibited subconscious of simple Viennese folk.

Stranitzky's contributions to the Old Viennese Popular Theater were not so much in the form of new themes, but rather in his fresh psychological interpretations of the comical in human beings. He was also responsible for developing a new dimension in the operatic material he employed for his plays.[12] Some aspects of the *Commedia dell'Arte* were still present. Love made the world go round, and intricately contrived misunderstandings served as catalysts for action. Comical elements in Stranitzky's musical comedy, which centered largely around the activities of Hanswurst, may not strike us as being funny today, as tastes in humor change from generation to generation.[13] His type of musical comedy emphasized extravagant scenery and extravagant technical design over rhetoric and meaningfulness. In his naïve, lovable manner, Hanswurst parodied and exposed the innate frailties of love, sex, pride, and the honorable intentions of the Viennese populace. Hanswurst was not a moralist; he neither accepted nor rejected the world around him, but simply insisted on asserting his innate right to exist.[14] A synthesis between Hanswurst and the Baroque world was to occur in later stages of the Old Viennese Popular Theater.

Stranitzky's language was generally pompous and extravagant and lacked the ability to communicate on a warm and personal

human level. This is reflected in the names of his musical comedies, which were in the form of double titles, as had been the
practice with the Jesuit Theater and the plays of travelling companies: *Triumph römischer Tugend und Tapferkeit oder Gordianus der Grosse.* (*Triumph of Roman Virtue and Bravery or
Gordianus the Great*). The *pièce de résistance,* however, was always the subtitle: "Mit Hanswurst, den lächerlichen Liebes-Am-
bassadeur, curiösen Befehlshaber, vermeinten Toten, ungeschick-
ten Mörder, gezwungenen Spion, und was noch mehr die Komödie
selbst erklären wird." ("With Hanswurst, the ridiculous ambassa-
dor of love, singular leader, presumed corpse, clumsy murderer,
forced spy, and other characteristics that will become evident in
the comedy.") Otto Rommel suggests that Stranitzky had not only
invested his Hanswurst with a new dimension in peasant humor
but that he also gave him more individual characteristics and a
more complicated pattern of behaviour than any of his precursors
had done.[15]

Stranitzky's successor, Gottfried Prehauser (1699–1769), received his initial training as a member of several travelling companies. He then joined Stranitzky's ensemble and became its head
in 1725. Prehauser's favorite role was that of Hanswurst, which
he played in the same manner as Stranitzky. Unlike his predeces-
sor, however, Prehauser was well educated and came from the
upper middle class. This personal background was reflected in the
comparatively greater moderation that characterized his plays.
Prehauser instituted a discernible refinement of grotesque and
crude elements that had prevailed in the early stages of the Old
Viennese Popular Theater. Infantilism gave way to an exuberant
form of adolescence. There was also a change in the language as
standard High German began to supplant the local Viennese dialect. Under Prehauser, Stranitzky's peasant-like and crude humor
acquired an urbane touch.

The structure of the musical comedies of the early Old Viennese
Popular Theater was very similar to that of the comic opera im-
ported from Italy. The Kärntnertor Theater became the home of
comic opera in the middle of the eighteenth century. Ballet and
folk dancing became integral elements of such performances. The
scenic design and the plot became increasingly complicated, re-
quiring sophisticated preparations. This in turn raised the ex-

penses of production. Although entrance fees had to be raised, the masses kept coming, for this was to them the ultimate in theater enjoyment.

Johann Josef Felix Kurz (1717–1784), better known as Bernardon, the name of the comical character he loved to depict, became Prehauser's competitor and eventually took over his job. Kurz came to the Kärntnertor Theater in 1737 at the age of twenty and quickly distinguished himself as an impulsive and boisterous actor. He was able to outdo Prehauser in braggadocio and magniloquence. After this early engagement in Vienna, Kurz formed his own acting company, with which he toured Prague, Warsaw, Venice, Munich, Nuremberg, Cologne, and many parts of Austria. After lengthy visits to these parts of Europe, Kurz returned to Vienna for the final triumph of his acting career.

The comical character made famous by Kurz was Bernardon, who followed in the footsteps of Hanswurst. He was to Kurz what Hanswurst had been to Stranitzky and Prehauser. Kurz was so successful in his portrayal of Bernardon, that people began referring to his plays as "Bernardoniades." The majority of these plays were adaptations of Italian operatic scores and *scenarii*.

Official censorship in the theater in Vienna resulted from the arguments concerning the place of Hanswurst alongside the classical theater. In 1751 the Empress Maria Theresia was pressured into issuing an edict which paved the way for the eventual removal of Hanswurst from the Imperial Court stage. The edict encouraged the production of plays from classical German, Spanish, French, and Italian literature. However, the majority of spectators still preferred Hanswurst to the complicated plots of the classics. Thus Hanswurst continued to reign in the guise of Bernardon.

In his lifetime Kurz wrote more than three hundred plays. Unconcerned with posterity, he wrote primarily for the tastes of contemporary audiences. His Bernardoniades were on the order of situation comedies, which became more imaginative as he grew older. Kurz is credited with the creation of the "Ambigue comique,"[16] a combination of comedy, pantomime and operetta. *Neue krumme Teufel* (*New Crooked Devils*) was one of the better-known examples of this genre, which he composed in collaboration with Josef Haydn. This popular tradition of Bernardoniades was continued in the plays of Friedrich Wilhelm Weiskern

(1711–1768), Johann Wilhelm Mayberg (1714–1761), and Franz Anton Nuth (1698–1794). Unfortunately, most of the plays authored by these three playwrights were not written down and have consequently been lost to posterity.

Philipp Hafner (1735–1764) has been called the father of the written Old Viennese Popular Theater. He was a master of the *Lokalstück* or local farce, which weeded out foreign influences and focused on the Viennese milieu. Because he did not explicitly teach public morality in his plays, he was considered suspect by the reformer Sonnenfels. The Viennese public, however, which was not particularly desirous of being preached to, continued to flock into the theater to see Hafner's plays. Hafner used such colorful pseudonyms as Kilian Fiedelbogen, Phakipfinpler, and Johanno Wurstio. In 1763, to poke fun at Sonnenfels, he wrote the play *Die reisenden Komödianten* (*Travelling Comedians*) and defended Hanswurst in a treatise entitled *Verteidigung der Wienerischen Schaubühne* (*In Defense of the Viennese Stage*).

Hafner's comedies maintain a close relationship with the *Commedia dell'Arte,* particularly in the names he used to designate his stock characters Odoardo and Colombine. Goethe found Hafner's comedies lively and interesting when he read an edition dedicated to him by a Viennese lady admirer.[17] Hafner's innovation in the development of the Old Viennese Popular Theater concerned the frequent use of local Viennese color and characters in his plays. This emphasis on typical local foibles and taboos made his fare irresistible to his audiences. Among his favorite plays were *Die bürgerliche Dame* (*The Bourgeois Lady*), *Etwas zum Lachen im Fasching* (*Something to Laugh about at Carnival Time*), *Evakathel und Schnudi,* and *Megära, die förchterliche Hexe* (*Megära, the Frightful Witch*). In this last play, Hanswurst appears side by side with Odoardo, Angela, and Colombine, who were borrowed from the *Commedia dell'Arte,* the lady magician Megära from the world of magic, and Leander, Riepel, and others from a typical Viennese milieu. Hafner's style paved the way for two subsequent imitators of his plays: Franz von Heufeld (1731–1795) and Christian Gottlieb Klemm (1736–1802).

Joachim Perinet (1765–1816), a long-time actor-playwright of the Leopoldstädter Theater, adapted many of Hafner's farces of Viennese life into musical comedies. Perinet was the author of more than a hundred plays. One of his most successful travesties was *Hamlet, der Prinz vom Tandelmarkt* (*Hamlet, Prince of the Rag-Fair*). Ferdinand Raimund appeared in Perinet's *Hamlet* during his early acting career, when he searched for tragic roles in which he could imitate his idol, the actor Ferdinand Ochsenheimer. A poet as well as a playwright, Perinet died a pauper at the age of fifty-one.

III   *The Suburban Theater*

With the death of Kurz and Prehauser, the Old Viennese Popular Theater moved its center of activity from the Kärntnertor Theater to the suburbs of Vienna. Travelling companies carried on the popular tradition upon improvised stages in the suburbs, where the majority of the lower classes lived. There existed many such stages in the suburbs. Some of them were torn down because they had become fire hazards, others were enlarged and rebuilt into permanent theaters.

The most important suburban theater that catered to the Old Viennese Popular Theater was the Leopoldstädter Theater. It was opened in 1781 under the actor-playwright Karl Marinelli (1744–1803), who succeeded Matthias Menninger as director of this ensemble. The first play was Marinelli's own, appropriately entitled *Aller Anfang ist schwer* (*All Beginning is Difficult*). The theater's star actor was Johann LaRoche (1745–1806), who hailed from Graz and had joined the ensemble in 1768. LaRoche became famous through the characterization of the comical character Kasperle, a relative of Bernardon and Hanswurst. Kasperle developed into a stock character, who was thoroughly Viennese in his outlook on life and in his general demeanor. Other outstanding actors of the early years of this ensemble included the brothers Johann, Ignaz, and Anton Sartory. When the Brünn Theater burned down mysteriously, its leading actor Anton Baumann joined the Leopoldstädter Theater, which was growing in fame from year to year.

The Leopoldstädter Theater's early leading resident playwright was Karl Friedrich Hensler (1759–1825), who authored some eighty plays between 1786 and 1803. He gave up writing after 1803 to devote full time to the management of this theater. He inherited some problems Marinelli had left behind. Among these was the settling of claims by the heirs of the theater owners. After LaRoche's death a suitable replacement had to be found for this comedian. Hensler also had to replace himself as playwright, in order to keep the insatiable Viennese public supplied with fresh material. Two of the resident playwrights at the Leopoldstädter Theater at that time were Joachim Perinet and Joseph Ferdinand Kringsteiner (1776–1810). Both contributed prolifically to the repertoire. The leading composer between 1786 and 1807 was Wenzel Müller, who had come to Vienna from Brünn. Another important author of musical comedies was Florian Leopold Gassmann (1729–1774).

Like Bernardon and Hanswurst before him, Kasperle appeared as a very versatile character on stage. He always took part in grandiose adventures and mixed with many unusual people in plays like *Wer anderen eine Grube gräbt, fällt selbst hinein* (*He who digs a hole for others falls into it himself*); *Junge Mädeln machen Sorgen* (*Young Maidens cause Trouble*); *Kasperl, der eifersüchtige Gärtner* (*Kasperl, the Jealous Gardner*); *Kaspar, der schläfrige Totenwächter* (*Kaspar, the exhausted Deathwatchman*). And who could resist a play with a title like this: *Der Witwer mit seinen Töchtern oder Mädeln wollen Männer: Ein sehr lustiges Stück in drei Aufzügen, wobei Kasperle als Friseur a la Mode, als Sesselträger, als Anstreicher, und als Stockmeister erscheint* (*Widower with daughters or Girls are after Men: A very funny story in three acts, in which Kasperle appears as a barber a la mode, a carrier of chairs, a painter, and an official charged with meting out corporal punishment*. The action of this kind of play was bizarre and led to impossible situations. This was precisely what the suburban audiences loved.

The Theater an der Wieden opened its doors in 1787 under the direction of actor-playwright Christian Rossback (1756–1793). It floundered under the management of the first few directors. When Emanuel Schikaneder (1751–1812) joined the management, the situation changed. He wrote the libretto for Mozart's *Zauberflöte* (*Magic Flute*), which was an instantaneous success. Schikaneder himself played the part of Papageno.

Born at Regensburg, Schikaneder entered upon his career as a wandering minstrel, and became a full-time actor at the age of twenty. By 1778 he had assumed directorship of his own company performing in various parts of Austria and Germany. During those years, Schikaneder met Mozart in Salzburg, where they became good friends. Well versed in the dramas of Goethe, Schiller, Lessing, and Shakespeare, he soon wrote plays of his own, which were heavily laced with typical situations from Viennese life: *Die Fiaker in Wien* (*The Hackney Coaches or Coachmen in Vienna*), *Der Fiaker in Baden* (*The Hackney Coach at Baden*) and *Der Tiroler Wastl* (*The Tyrolean Wastl*). Wastl was a comical relative of Kasperle, Bernardon, and Hanswurst. A very popular fairy-tale play was his *Schembera, Herr von Boskovitz*, which showed a distinct relationship to the chapbook of *Faust*. Schikaneder desperately and vainly wanted to repeat the success of the *Magic Flute* with such operatic works as *Der Spiegel von Arkadien* (*The Mirror of Arcadia*), *Der Königssohn aus Ithaka* (*The Prince from Ithaca*), and *Babylons Pyramiden* (*Babylon's Pyramids*).

When the Theater an der Widen was to be closed by the authorities because it had become a fire hazard, Schikaneder had no difficulty gathering financial backers to reopen this theater on June 13, 1801, as the Theater an der Wien. Having rebuilt it, the Theater an der Wien became one of the biggest and most beautiful theaters in Vienna. The new stage was large enough to hold up to five hundred people and more than fifty horses at one time. One of the most popular attractions was the production of the opera *Babylons Pyramiden*, which contained elaborate castles, grand parades, animal scenes, appearances of ghosts, and many other sensational features.

The third significant theater in suburban Vienna was the Josefstädter Theater, which opened its doors on October 29, 1788, under the management of actor-director Karl Mayer (1750–1830). He inherited the ensemble of the Franz Scherzer acting company, which held forth at the Bauernfeind Hall and included in its repertory plays by Hafner, Kurz and Shakespeare. Johann Michael Köck, a rich entrepreneur and innkeeper in the Viennese suburb of Josefstadt, had built the Josefstädter Theater for his son-in-law Karl Mayer. However, Mayer soon lost interest in the theater and leased it to a number of generally incompetent managers.

Two of the resident playwrights of the Josefstädter Theater during its early period were Matthäus Voll (1759–1822) and

Ferdinand Eberl (1762–1805). Eberl was the better known of the two and wrote such popular plays as *Das listige Stubenmädchen* (*The Cunning Chamber Maid*), 1784; *Die Limonadehütte* (*The Lemonade Hut*), 1793; and *Der Eipeldauer am Hofe* (*The Eipeldauer at Court*), 1797. Elberl tried his hand at managing the theater between 1795 and 1796, but he soon found out that he could not handle the job.

The attractive dancer Maria Medina Vigano was engaged by the Josefstädter Theater in an attempt to get publicity for its activities. She soon became the rage of Vienna as she danced on stage dressed in a suggestive flesh-colored tricot. The theater soon engaged a second dancer, who was younger, also called herself Vigano, and imitated the older Vigano in her mannerisms and dancing. The audiences were divided into those who preferred the original Vigano and those who liked the younger Vigano. In his memoirs, Adolf Bäuerle states that he himself preferred the younger one because he found her charming not only on stage but also after her performances.[18]

The grandest performance of 1803 was Christian Albrecht Gottfried's much heralded *Der Todesreiter* (*The Death Rider*). The play opened with great fanfare and featured flying objects, fireworks, and other fantastic stage effects designed to entice the audiences. Gottfried's other popular plays included *O, du lieber Augustin, alles ist hin* (*Oh, dear Augustin, all is gone*), *Der hundertäugige Argos* (*Argos with a hundred Eyes*), and *Das Turnier im Kalmückenland* (*The Tournament in the Land of the Kalmucks*), an adaptation of Philipp Hafner's play by the same name.

In 1812 Karl Mayer, the owner of the Josefstädter Theater, leased it to Josef Huber, the brother of Leopold Huber who managed the Leopoldstädter Theater. Huber had little previous training in theater management and did not distinguish himself in his new capacity. However, he did write some moderately successful plays, among them *Das Haustheater* (*The Domestic Theater*), *Die beiden Linzerinnen* (*The Two Women from Linz*) and *Die Frau Resel aus Steiermark* (*Styria's Mrs. Resel*). Perhaps Josef Huber's greatest single accomplishment was his engagement of the playwright Alois Gleich and the promising young actor Ferdinand Raimund.

The years that followed saw the engagement of the popular

comedian Wenzel Scholz, who had moved to Vienna from Graz, and whose presence raised the level of performances at the Josefstädter Theater. The playwright Johann Nepomuk Nestroy made his acting debut at this theater in 1829 in his own play, *Die Verbannung aus dem Zauberreiche oder Dreissig Jahre aus dem Leben eines Lumpen* (*The Banishment from the Fairy-tale World or Thirty Years from the Life of a Rascal*). Under Johann Stöger's direction, the Josefstädter Theater began to include also operas in its regular repertory, thus competing in that field with the Kärntnertor Theater. Eventually the mixed and versatile repertory included popular farces, operas, and musical comedies. World acclaim came to the Josefstädter Theater when Max Reinhardt (1873–1943) assumed the management in 1923.

IV *The Big Three*

The three playwrights of the Old Viennese Popular Theater who dominated the Viennese stages between 1780 and 1825 were Adolf Bäuerle (1786–1859), Joseph Alois Gleich (1772–1841), and Carl Meisl (1775–1853). They continued on a higher literary level the tradition that was started by Stranitzky, Prehauser, and Hafner. The written output of these three playwrights was tremendous: Bäuerle authored some eighty plays, Meisl one hundred and seventy, and Gleich over two hundred. Few of these plays will go down in literary history. Nor was playwriting the only profession in which these three men engaged. Their plays were written primarily for their impact on the Viennese, who came into the theater to be entertained. In order to achieve this purpose, these plays had to be uncomplicated and dwell upon familiar themes. To make such themes palatable to the audiencs, new gimmicks were constantly added.

Bäuerle, Gleich, and Meisl were very popular with the Viennese public. Somewhat less popular, though still frequently performed, were the plays of August Kotzebue and August Wilhelm Iffland, who specialized in sentimental and bourgeois dramas. Goethe, Schiller, Shakespeare, and Calderón were also held in great respect by the Viennese populace; however, the situations and problems their dramas portrayed seemed beyond their scope of understanding. To make these classics comprehensible, playwrights of the Old Viennese Popular Theater wrote parodies of these works, which usually simplified the plots and poked fun at unlikely situations. The tradition of the Old Viennese Popular Theater popularized not only the masterpieces of world drama, but also the mythology of the Romans and Greeks. The most popular dramatic form was that of the *Lokalposse,* which generated a new comical character created by Bäerle. This comical character was Staberl, a relative of Kasperl, Bernardon, and Hanswurst. The next most popular genre was the *Zauberstück* or popular magic comedy, which continued the extravagant Baroque tradition.

Carl Meisl (1775–1853) was born in Laibach and attended the University of Lemberg before settling down in Vienna. At home in all the genres of the Old Viennese Popular Theater tradition, he was also the most prolific of the three leading playwrights. In 1801 Meisl made his debut at the Leopoldstädter Theater with the robber story *Carolo Carolini.* Shortly thereafter this play was also given at the Josefstädter Theater and the Theater an der Wien, a pattern that was frequently repeated with Meisl's other plays, as well as those of his colleagues Bäuerle and Gleich. Meisl was somewhat skeptical by nature and wrote satires and parodies in addition to essays and poetry. When Grillparzer did not deliver a commissioned historical play intended for the coronation ceremonies of Empress Karoline as Queen of Hungary in 1825, Meisl assumed the task in a few short days and wrote *Gisela von Bayern, erste Königin der Magyaren* (*Gisela of Bavaria, First Queen of the Hungarians*). This feat earned him honors and good money.[19]

Meisl started his writing career with comedies about knighthood and plays about personages from history and mythology. He had no great drive for originality and frequently used the well known themes of others and adapted them to the Viennese milieu. In a similar manner he took Kringsteiner's *Orpheus und Euridice,* retained its title and made it into a popular success. Whenever Meisl depicted situations and characters from mythology, he felt free to change basic circumstances, usually adding new motives and acclimatizing the characters and situations to life in Vienna. Olympian gods and members of the Viennese populace mixed freely in Meisl's plays. These gods usually had much more fun when they consorted with the amiable Viennese than with their own kind. Amor was one of the few unhappy gods in Vienna, who felt that he was being put out of business by the new mercenary spirit that was sweeping the country. Sisyphus can be found working in a labor gang, and the Devil himself is forced to take the customary coffee break, thus giving the sinners a breather from their eternal tortures. Meisl particularly delighted in ridiculing contrived situations in the works of classical authors by suggesting that their impenetrability was probably due to their highly profound nature.

Ferdinand Raimund's portrayal of Fritz in Meisl's *Der lustige Fritz oder Schlaf, Traum und Besserung* (*Merry Fritz, or Sleep, Dream, and Recuperation*) turned it into a popular success. This play was a parody of Karl Franz van der Velde's play by the same name. Shortly after Meisl's version scored a success, Franz Xaver Told von Doldenburg (1789–1849) produced a parody of it entitled *Der traurige Fritz, oder schlafe, träume, stehe auf, kleide dich an und sei lustig.* (*The Sad Fritz, or Sleep, Dream, Get Up, Get Dressed, and Be Merry*), which also became a favorite of the Viennese audiences. The actor Fritz Wimmer from the Josefsädter Theater wrote a parody of Told von Doldenburg's parody of Meisl's play, which was itself a parody of van der Velde's original. Wimmer's parody was entitled *Der närrische Fritz oder Schlafe, träume, stehe auf, kleide dich an und sei gescheit* (*Foolish Fritz, or Sleep, Dream, Get up, Get dressed, and Be Smart*) and was produced in 1819. Paolo Rainoldi then wrote a pantomime on the same subject. Franz Xaver Told von Doldenburg wrote other parodies that were very popular, among them a parody of Grillparzer's *Sappho,* which he called *Sepherl* and converted entirely into a Viennese milieu. Grillparzer's *Der Traum ein Leben* (*The Dream, a Life*) became *Das Leben ein Rausch* (*Life as Intoxication*), and Schiller's *Die Jungfrau von Orleans* (*Maiden of Orleans*) became *Die Jungfrau von Oberlans* (*Maiden of Oberlans*).

Meisl's association with the Leopoldstädter Theater lasted from 1801 to 1817. It was there that he experienced his greatest successes and his greatest failures. After 1822 he wrote primarily for the Josefstädter Theater. Meisl's last magic comedy was *Das grüne Männchen oder Der Vater von dreizehn Töchtern* (*The Green Manikin or The Father of Thirteen Daughters*), which was derived from one of Grimm's fairy-tales. Meisl's parody of Raimund's *Moisasurs Zauberspruch,* which he called *Moisasuras*

Hexenspruch oder die Zerstörung des Kaffeetempels (*Moisasura's Witches' Sayings or the Destruction of the Coffee Temple*), was rejected by the public, although it was not completely without redeeming features.

Additional plays by Meisl that proved successful with the Viennese public included *Die Entführung der Prinzessin Europa oder So geht's im Olympus* (*Seduction of Princess Europe or That's how Things are on Mount Olympus*), *Das Gespenst auf der Bastei* (*The Ghost on the Bastion*), with its sequels *Das Gespenst in der Familie* (*The Ghost in the Family*), *Das Gespenst im Prater* (*The Ghost in the Prater*), and *Des Wanderers Ziel* (*Wanderer's Goal*). Equally popular were Meisl's parodies of Raimund's *Der Verschwender*, which he called *Der Streitmacher* (*The Quarrelsome Fellow*), and *Werthers Leiden* (*Werther's Sorrows*), a parody of Kringsteiner's play by that name.[20]

Adolf Bäuerle (1786–1859) was the most popular and precocious of the three playwrights. At sixteen he wrote his first novel, at seventeen he became a newspaper editor, at eighteen he married his first wife, at nineteen he wrote his first comedy, and at twenty he became editor of the prestigious "Wiener Theaterzeitung," a position he held from 1806 to 1859. Well educated, Bäuerle was the son of a wealthy factory owner. His first job was that of a clerk in the Government. He became an admirer of the writings of Kotzebue, Hafner, Schikaneder, Hensler, Gleich, and Kringsteiner. The first play he wrote, and one of the most successful ones, was *Die Bürger in Wien* (*The Bourgeois of Vienna*), which was produced in October, 1813, at the Leopoldstädter Theater. It depicted the story of a simple craftsman who refused to allow his daughter to marry an inferior poet. When the poet performs a feat of heroism, however, the craftsman changes his mind and gives his blessing to the marriage. This play made theatrical history because of the first appearance of Staberl, who was Bäuerle's version of the stock comical character. The popular actor Ignaz Schuster developed and perfected the character of Staberl, who was a typical Viennese character thriving on his singular interpretations of Viennese life and foibles. Ludwig Tieck was strongly impressed with Schuster's acting ability.[21] Most of the leading actors of that day, among them Raimund, Nestroy,

[38]

Kringsteiner, and Wenzel Scholz, impersonated Staberl. It was up to each actor to imbue him with an amiable personality and disposition. The humorous effect depended upon Staberl's ability to parody the peculiarities and sacred institutions of the Viennese.

Besides Local Viennese farces, Bäuerle also wrote magic comedies. One of the better examples of this genre was *Doktor Fausts Mantel* (*Doctor Faust's Overcoat*), with music by Wenzel Müller, which became an instantaneous hit. In 1825, theater director Carl, whose real name was Karl Andreas von Bernbrunn (1789-1854), adapted Bäuerle's play and called it *Fausts Mantel oder Staberl in Floribus* (*Faust's Overcoat or Staberl in the Flowers*). Bäuerle wrote a companion piece entitled *Der Schatten von Fausts Weibe* (*The Shadow of Faust's Wife*), in which Faust is also saved from eternal damnation. The Viennese public appreciated the humane ending of Bäuerle's Faust, since previous renditions had insisted on sending him to hell.

Like his fellow playwrights, Bäuerle also wrote a number of parodies. His parody of Rossini's opera *Tancredi* retained the name of the original but had a new musical score by Wenzel Müller. It was performed at the Leopoldstädter Theater and was well received by the public. This moved Gleich to write a parody of the parody, entitled *Der neue Tankredi* (*The New Tankredi*), which was given at the Josefstädter Theater. Some parodies became more popular than their originals. This was the case with Bäuerle's *Aline oder Wien in einem anderen Weltteil* (*Aline or Vienna in Another Continent*), which was based on François Berton's opera *Aline*. In his parody, which was performed in 1822, Bäuerle had moved the locale to Vienna and changed Aline from a Neapolitan farm girl into a Viennese middle class maiden. Some of the Viennese who had seen Berton's opera thought that they finally understood it after seeing Bäuerle's simplified version. To Bäuerle and his fellow playwrights, no masterpiece was too sacred.

Another popular play by Bäuerle was *Wien, Paris, London, und Konstantinopel*, first produced in 1823. It depicted a journey to all these famous cities, concluding, however, that after all was said and done, none of them could measure up to Vienna: "Drum wir werden, sagen s', nit mehr weiter gehn, denn in Wien, sagen s', ist's doch gar zu schön." ("Therefore, we are not going to travel on, because it's pleasant enough in Vienna"), the chorus sings at the end of the play.

Der Mann mit Millionen, schön, jung, und doch nicht glücklich (*The Millionaire, Handsome, Young, and Yet Unhappy*) is a play that could be produced today with a bit of sprucing up, and it might be as popular as in 1829. In his parody of Schiller's *Kabale und Liebe* (*Intrigue and Love*), Bäuerle made Lady Milfort into a very marriageable character from the world of fairies. This play owed its success to Raimund's characterization of the musician Miller and Katharina Ennöckl's portrayal of the fairy Millifort.[22] Bäuerle was also a noted novelist. Writing under various pseudonyms, he depicted well-known persons and events from the Viennese milieu which he himself helped to shape. Among these were *Therese Krones* in 1851, *Aus den Geheimnissen eines Wiener Advokaten* (*From the Secret Files of a Viennese Lawyer*) in 1854, and his most popular, *Ferdinand Raimund* (1855), which was a partly true and partly fictional treatment of the life and work of one of Vienna's favorite sons.

The third playwright who dominated the Viennese stage between 1780 and 1830 was Joseph Alois Gleich (1772–1841). After graduation from the University of Vienna, he worked for a while as a government official. His literary career started around 1791 and lasted until 1830. Between 1804 and 1811 he was resident playwright at the Leopoldstädter Theater, and between 1819 and 1828 at the Josefstädter Theater. Throughout most of his life he was in debt and at the mercy of creditors. Once Gleich even arranged for the seduction of his fourteen-year-old daughter by the urbane and wealthy Prince Wenzel Anton Kaunitz.[23] He was largely responsible for the shotgun wedding between his daughter Luise and Ferdinand Raimund. To earn the money necessary for the kind of living to which he was accustomed, he wrote voluminously. In addition to the more than two hundred plays, he produced over one hundred novels under such pseudonyms as Bergenstamm, Adolf Blum, Dellarosa, and H. Walden.

Gleich's first play was *Elizabeth, Gräfin von Hochfeld* (*Elizabeth, Countess of Hochfeld*), a story of knighthood, first produced in 1791. The first plays Gleich wrote as a resident playwright at the Leopoldstädter Theater were historical: *Die Löw-*

enritter (*The Lion's Knights*), *Der Hungerturm* (*Hungertower*), and *Die Fürsten der Langobarden* (*The Princes of the Lombards*). The genre of Romantic fairy-tale plays, with a touch of the Viennese spirit, was another favorite of Gleich's: *Der Mann vom Kahlenberg* (*The Man from Kahlenberg*), and *Die vier Heymons-Kinder* (*The Four Heymon Children*). Gleich was extremely well read in history, which he tried to popularize for the Viennese. Historical plays, adapted to Viennese customs, included *Die eiserne Jungfrau* (*The Iron Maiden*), *Aragis von Benevent*, and *Leopolds Jagd oder Der wiedergefundene Schleier* (*Leopold's Hunt or The Retrieved Veil*). Gleich wrote prolifically about the Burgundians, the Franks, the Vandals, the Lombards, the Prussians, and the Venetians—all of whom came to look and talk like the typical Viennese. This kind of homespun wisdom amused the Viennese bourgeoisie, which was thus convinced that it had all along been in the best of all possible worlds. Occasionally Gleich adapted the plays of his predecessors in the Old Viennese Popular Theater tradition. His two adaptations from Kringsteiner, *Haus in Wien* (*A House in Vienna*) and *Haus in der Heimat* (*A House in One's Native Country*), spruced up with a few new jokes, were moderately successful. One of Gleich's most successful parodies was *Fiesko, der Salami-Krämer*, poking fun at Schiller's *Fiesko*, which was in those days frequently given at the Burgtheater. Gleich's Fiesko is not a Genoese nobleman, but rather a Viennese sausage maker, and the play deals with life among Viennese sausage makers. The importance these sausage makers ascribe to themselves surpasses by far the prerogatives claimed by Schiller's Fiesko. And their wives feel that they have reached utter sophistication when they come to the conclusion that the atention they sometimes receive from strangers is solely a prelude to seduction.

After studying the various talents of the young actor Ferdinand Raimund, Gleich wrote a play especially suited for him. This was *Adam Kratzerl von Kratzerlsfeld*, a sequel to his *Die Musikanten am Hohenmarkt* (*The Musicians from Hohenmarkt*), in which Raimund had played a role. Raimund became a star actor with his portrayal of Kratzerl, who was the latest relative of Staberl and Kasperl. However, Kratzerl was more versatile than his predecessors, as he played the violin; and with each succeeding play in the cycle he rose in Viennese society. Other plays in the Kratzerl cycle include *Herr Adam Kratzerl und sein Pudel* (*Mr. Adam Kratzerl and his Poodle*) and *Herr Kratzerl und seine Familie* (*Mr. Kratzerl and his Family*).

Another genre that appealed to Gleich was the *Besserungsstück* or play suggesting the improvement of manners and habits. Somewhat didactic, though usually humorous, this category includes his *Der Eheteufel auf Reisen* (*The Marriage Devil Abroad*) and its equally well-received *Der Eheteufel in der Heimat* (*The Marriage Devil at Home*). The basic plot concerns a connoisseur of wives and wenches. Ferdinand Raimund had initially appeared in the title role of the Marriage Devil, which he made famous through his ability to change from one character to another in his efforts to entrap the weaker sex. Other plays of the same genre by Gleich included *Der Hölle Zaubergaben* (*Hell's Magic Gifts*), and *Die Schauernacht im Felsentale* (*The Night of Horror in the Garden of Rocks*).

Gleich's most notorious play was *Der Pächter und der Tod* (*The Tenant Farmer and Death*), which was inspired by Meisl's *Gespenst auf der Bastei*. This play caused a scandal when people complained about the derogatory depiction of "Death" on stage. The police commissioner eventually prevailed upon Gleich to change "Death" into a more abstract "Doorkeeper of Pluto." The plot deals with Philemon, who, with the help of magic and some clever arguments, twice forced Death to prolong his life by another five hundred years. Even Philemon had to die in the end, but not before he had caused a great deal of mischief. To assuage the ruffled feelings of some spectators and the police, Gleich also changed the title to the more innocuous *Pächter Valentin* (Tenant Farmer Valentin). Raimund considered the part of Valentin one of his favorite roles.[24]

V   *The Period of Maturity*

The golden era of the Old Viennese Popular Theater comprises primarily the work of Ferdinand Raimund (1790–1836) and Johann Nepomuk Nestroy (1801–1862). Still related to the tradition of the Old Viennese Popular Theater, though lacking its effervescent spark and naïveté, was the work of Franz Grillparzer (1791–1872) and Ludwig Anzengruber (1839–1889).

Raimund was orphaned early in life and had to make his way to the top of his profession without the aid of a university education. He was in every sense a self-made man. Nestroy, on the other hand, came from a well-to-do family and received a fine university education. In his work and in his outlook on life, Raimund tended to be a late product of the Baroque and Romantic eras, whereas Nestroy was more a precursor of Realism. Half a year older than his idol Grillparzer, Raimund was convinced that he was born to be a tragedian, but he was most successful as a comedian. Nestroy wanted to be a comedian, but was more convincing in roles that were serious, analytical, or satirical.

Raimund's first big chance in life came when he joined the ensemble of the Josefstädter Theater where he mixed with the leading playwrights of the Old Viennese Popular Theater and with some of the most versatile actors of his day. Highly demanding of women, Raimund was never completely happy with them. His marriage to the wild and undomesticated Luise Gleich was brief and painful. His relations with Toni Wagner, too, became sometimes strained because of misunderstandings and fits of jealousy. By nature very sensitive to the outside world, Raimund frequently despaired of the intrigues and injustices that surrounded him. The world of the theater was a haven from the problems of everyday life. When things did not work out at the theater, Raimund withdrew into himself and went through periods of melancholy and depression.

Raimund became a playwright by accident. He started out by writing inserts consisting of jokes and new incidents for the plays in which he performed. Then, accepting the advice of friends, Raimund composed his own plays. In his first two plays, he stuck closely to the traditional form of the Old Viennese Popular Theater. Although the comedies of Gleich, Bäuerle, and Meisl were not always of the highest literary quality, they had an effervescence normally associated with plays intended for the general populace. Thus Raimund followed his predecessors in the style and technique of his first two plays, *Der Barometermacher auf der Zauberinsel* in 1823, and *Der Diamant des Geisterkönigs* in 1824.

However, Raimund did not long stay satisfied with working according to prescription. He wanted to improve his own writing and the level of the traditional Old Viennese Popular Theater. He had shown an unmistakable drive to excel as an actor, and now he wanted to excel also as a playwright. His third play, *Das Mädchen aus der Feenwelt oder Der Bauer als Millionär,* deviated from the standard fare by becoming a profound human story about the life of the farmer-millionaire Fortunatus Wurzel. The philosophical basis of this play is Raimund's own conviction that most human beings, including Fortunatus Wurzel, are able to understand the significance of material wealth as opposed to the importance of human happiness only when they themselves have not been touched by the corrupting force of money. This theme was of universal interest to the Viennese populace because the country had only recently gone through periods of war, inflation, and prosperity in comparatively quick order.

With each new play Raimund attempted to improve upon his previous one. The real and imagined disappointments in his life led him to seek a better world in his plays, where justice and beauty could prevail as was impossible in the world of reality. He wanted to make this vision available to his audiences in order to convince them of the possiblity of a world that was saner than the one they were accustomed to. With *Der Alpenkönig und der Menschenfeind,* Raimund rose to the level of Molière and Shakespeare. Rooted in the tradition of the Old Viennese Popular Theater, this play contains elements of illusion and reality, fact and fiction, and sophisticated humane entertainment. It is the story of the misanthrope Rappelkopf, who gains a better perspective of himself and the world around him when he encounters his double image. Raimund employs elements of magic to secure better understanding where the human element seems to fail.

Raimund's last play, *Der Verschwender,* was also his most popular one. Although he originally addressed himself primarily to Viennese audiences, his deep compassion and understanding of the human condition gave his work universal significance. Originally regarded as a local playwright, he has, in the meantime, been elevated to classical status by being performed at the venerable Burgtheater, along with Shakespeare and the Greek tragedies.

As Realism began to triumph in the theater, it gave rise to scepticism. Endowed with a critical mind, Johann Nepomuk Nestroy (1801–1862), dominated the Viennese stage after Raimund's death. For many years the Viennese had not been permitted to express doubt about the various forms of corruption in their Establishment. Thus, when Nestroy appeared upon the horizon, he was welcomed by the public for his sardonic wit and cynical attitude towards the Viennese way of life.

Nestroy made his stage debut as an operatic singer at the Hofoperntheater in Vienna. Although he had earned a law degree at the University of Vienna, he never practiced that profession. In 1823 he married the former Wilhelmine Nespiesni and moved to Amsterdam, where he gained invaluable stage experience and earned more money than at home in Vienna. While in Amsterdam, he appeared in as many as fifty-two different roles.[25] The majority of these were singing roles in the operas of Mozart, Rossini, and in Beethoven's *Fidelio*. When the Amsterdam Theater folded, Nestroy returned to Vienna via Brünn and Graz, two cities with flourishing theaters.

Back in Vienna in 1831, Nestroy changed from singing to speaking roles. He appeared as Gessler in Schiller's *Wilhelm Tell*, as Burleigh in *Maria Stuart*, as Bildau in Iffland's *Spieler*, and even as Kasperle in Hensler's *Teufelsmühle am Wienerberg* (*Devil's Mill on the Wienerberg*). One of his great weaknesses was that he loved to extemporize, which led to difficulties with theater managements and the police.

As Nestroy reacquainted himself with the Old Viennese Popular Theater, Gleich and other playwrights began writing roles especially intended for his talents. Gleich's *Ydor, der Wanderer* and Meisl's *Der Eheteufel auf Reisen* were two such plays written for Nestroy. Nestroy was also interested in Raimund's plays, which were then dominating the Viennese stage. He played some of the roles Raimund had written for himself, except that his interpretation was radically different from that of their creator. This infuriated Raimund when he found out about it. Raimund refused further performance rights to theaters which employed Nestroy to act in the leading roles of his plays. In those days, the author retained control over all performances of his plays, as long as he did not publish them. Raimund felt that he was forced to take this action because Nestroy insisted on "misinterpreting" his character roles.

Eventually Nestroy decided to write his own plays. He had written his first one before his return to Vienna, while he was engaged at the Graz Theater. It was a benefit play for himself, entitled *Die Verbannung aus dem Zauberreiche oder Dreissig Jahre aus dem Leben eines Lumpen (Banishment from the Magic World or Thirty Years from the Life of a Rascal)*, which was premiered at Graz in 1828. Nestroy liked variety and appeared not only in his own plays but also in many others. In his thirty years as an actor in Vienna, he reputedly appeared in no less than eight hundred and seventy-nine different roles.[26] He himself wrote about seventy plays.[27] The public's favorites were *Lumpazivagabundus, Die verhängnisvolle Faschingsnacht* (The Fatal Carnival Night), *Die beiden Nachtwandler (The Two Sleepwalkers), Mädl aus der Vorstadt (Girl from the Suburb), Einen Jux will er sich machen (He Wants to Go on a Spree)*, and Der Zerrissene (*The Shattered Man*). Nestroy's most popular parody was that of Friedrich Hebbel's *Judith und Holofernes*, in which Holofernes tries to outdo himself; ". . . noch hab' ich keine Schlacht verloren; ich bin die Jungfrau unter den Feldern. Ich möchte mich einmal mit mir selbst zusammenhetzen, nur um zu sagen, wer stärker ist: ich oder ich." ("I have never yet lost a battle, I'm a virgin among military leaders. Just once I'd like to fight with myself, so that I am able to tell who is stronger: I or I." When he exhausted Austrian and German sources for his plays, Nestroy turned to the French Comédie-Vaudeville. His *Die Papiere des Teufels (The Devil's Papers)* is based on Etienne Arago's and Paul Vermond's *Les mémoires du diable*.

A fate similar to Raimund's befell Nestroy at the end of his acting career. During Raimund's last years, Nestroy grew in popularity and threatened to overshadow him. This caused Raimund great grief. In Nestroy's old age, there appeared the comedian-playwright Karl Treumann (1823–1877), whose popularity began to rival that of his mentor. Treumann had come from Hamburg and joined the Carl Theater, where he associated with Nestroy. Both served in the capacity of actor-director-playwright. After a six-year period as director of the Carl Theater, Nestroy resigned his position in 1860 and went into retirement at Graz. There he died of a heart attack in 1862. For a number of years after his death, most of Nestroy's plays vanished from the repertory of Viennese theaters. This occurred because many actors did not dare to play the roles he had made famous. This attitude changed around 1881, when the Carl Theater began to revive his plays.

The two other playwrights who were associated with the Old Viennese Popular Theater tradition were Franz Grillparzer and Ludwig Anzengruber. Grillparzer's *Weh dem der lügt* (*Woe to Him Who Lies*), with its naïve and fairly-like atmosphere, was closely akin to Raimund and Shakespeare. Eventually, however, Grillparzer's theatrical genius expanded to new poetic horizons, and he became Austria's greatest dramatist.

Some of Anzengruber's characters, such as Gerbersepp (Tanner Joe), and Wurzelsepp (Rootdigger Joe) in *Der Pfarrer von Kirchfeld* (*The Priest from Kirchfeld*) were distant relatives of Kratzerl, Staberl, and Kasperl. They were more extensively developed as characters, and showed a touch of rustic Austrian peasantry. In his later plays Anzengruber became too much of a realist to fit into the mold of the traditional Old Viennese Popular Theater, although the roots of his works had unmistakably been nourished there.

With the death of Nestroy, the tradition of the Old Viennese Popular Theater had come to an end. It received its *coup de grâce* when Realism was in the ascendancy. The technological revolution began to lure people away from a naïve magic world which was no longer in tune with the verities of the time. The modern Viennese look at the Old Viennese Popular Theater tradition as a gem of the past that no longer completely fits the sceptical and analytical twentieth century. However, there is a universal appeal in the plays of Raimund and Nestroy, which has placed them in the repertory of European theaters to this day.

CHAPTER 2

Acting, Directing—Apprenticeship to Playwriting

RAIMUND wanted to become an actor ever since he set foot in the theater in his early teens. Since acting was not considered a very respectable profession, he experienced strong opposition from his father. Coming from a working-class family, his father wanted him to rise above that class. He was angered that his son was in no way to be dissuaded from becoming an actor. At first he lectured his son about the low status and godless nature of acting; later, warnings and curses were added. While on his deathbed, an anecdote has it, the father saw Ferdinand in the next room, in front of a mirror, practising various facial expressions he had acquired from his idol, the actor Ferdinand Ochsenheimer (1767–1822) at the Burgtheater. Utterly shocked by this sight, the father cursed Ferdinand in case he should go through with his intention of becoming an actor. This curse seemed to haunt Ferdinanad Raimund all his life. But it did not keep him from entering the acting profession. Since 1807 his idol Ochsenheimer was a popular character actor at the Burgtheater, where he specialized in roles of intriguers and tragic characters. He was not only an actor, but also an amateur dramatist.[1] Raimund desperately wanted to be like his idol and proceeded to adopt Ochsenheimer's gestures and mannerisms.

I *Novice Thespian: 1808–1814*

After his father's death in 1804, Raimund went to live with his sister Anna. Since his sister's family was not too well off, he had to take a job as an apprentice in a bakery. In addition to working there, he also sold candy and liquid refreshments at the Burgtheater. When the lights were dimmed and the performance had begun, Raimund allowed his imagination to transport him into another world, filled with wonderful adventures. He was particularly entranced when Ochsenheimer performed. The longer he observed Ochsenheimer on stage, the greater became his desire to become an actor. Thus, one day in 1808, he left his job and the security of living at the home of his sister, and set out to pursue his goal. He left Jung's bakery with the following farewell expressed in Viennese dialect: "Diese vierzig Nuss' sind meine letzte Buss." [2] ("These forty nuts constitute my last bit of penance.")

Raimund's features displayed no special characteristics. He probably never stood out in a crowd. Rolling his "r's" was a difficult task for him, and he always spoke in a hasty, almost incomprehensible manner. All these shortcomings, however, did not discourage him from venturing out into the uncertain world of travelling theater companies that played outside Vienna. It was not so much his natural talent as his strong willpower that made him persist in his drive. Aware of his shortcomings as an actor, Raimund accepted without pay every role he could lay his hands on. Those were sometimes bitter days of hunger and deprivation.

At the Meidling Theater, Raimund flunked his first audition, when director Kralitschek discovered that he could not roll his "r's" and had a tendency toward mumbling. At the Pressburg Theater, he was booed off the stage by an impatient and ungracious audience. At Steinamanger he was allowed to perform with Hain's Theater Company until he was fired. These setbacks dimmed his expectations of the acting profession, but not enough to want to abandon it. Director Christoph Kuntz, who managed the Ödenburg and Raab Theaters, was the first person who sensed Raimund's talents as an actor and allowed him to make mistakes while learning. Since he didn't pay Raimund very much, he was able to make a profit into the bargain.

Raimund's first documented performance on stage took place on March 5, 1810, when he appeared as the locksmith Hämmerling in Leopold Huber's popular fairy-tale play, *Der eiserne Mann oder die Drudenhöhle im Wienerwald* (*The Iron Man or The Witch's Den in the Vienna Woods*) with the Felix Frasel Theater Company at Ödenburg.[3] Another appearance took place on October 13, 1811, when Raimund appeared as Rochus Pumpernickel in Matthäus Stegmayer's play *Pumpernickels Hochzeitstag* (*Pum-*

pernickel's Wedding Day) under the direction of Christoph Kuntz. The young thespian also performed in 1813 in Josef Ferdinand Kringsteiner's comic opera *Die schwarze Redoute* (*The Black Masquerade*). In the same year he played the part of Antenor in August Kotzebue's *Arete, oder Kindestreue* (*Arete, or a Child's Loyalty*).

Around this time Raimund was surrounded by attractive young women, off and on stage, and could not resist falling in love with most of them. He always idealized the women he loved, and became very exasperated when he discovered that they were made of flesh and blood and had all the weaknesses common to the sex. This exasperation with the mortal variety of womanhood led him several times to half-hearted attempts at suicide. Once, upon being fished out of the cold river after one such attempt, he is said to have muttered: "Man kann sich doch nicht in einem fort umbringen!" ("One can't kill oneself all the time!")

II   *Engagements in Vienna: 1814–1830*

With the help of his friend, the actor Josef Kindler, Raimund came to the attention of director at the Josefstädter Theater, Josef Huber, who gave the young actor his first job in Vienna. In his autobiography, Raimund states that he felt he was born to be an actor of tragic roles; however, each time he appeared in a tragic role, he elicited loud laughter from his audiences.[4] He made his first appearance at the Josefstädter Theater in April or May, 1814,[5] in the part of the tenant farmer Feldkümmel in August Kotzebue's comedy *Pächter Feldkümmels Hochzeitstag* (*Tenant Farmer Feldkümmel's Wedding Day*). Shortly thereafter he appeared as Franz Moor in Schiller's tragedy *Die Räuber* (*The Robbers*). Adolf Bäuerle's "Wiener Theaterzeitung" reported that Raimund was copying Ochsenheimer in every respect, and that it might be to his advantage to develop a style of his own.[6] Other newspapers argued that great actors begin their careers by copying models.

More than a year later, on August 3, 1815, Raimund was invited by Leopold Huber to make a guest appearance at the Leopoldstädter Theater, then the leading suburban theater in Vienna. He appeared as Prince Schnudi in Joachim Perinet's adaptation of Philipp Hafner's *Evakathel und Schnudi*. It was here that he met

Schuster. He felt that I
ality and empathy. S
were calling Raimund
In 1891 Raimund m
They soon fell in love.
ever, her parents obje
listen, she was uncer
distant relatives outsid
broken. The actress L
back to health. There
Prince Alois Wenzl K
Raimund knew what l
Luise. She was a disap
"Aber beissen—am H
Viech umbringen!" ("(
day! This is the height-
ordeal!") A few montl
girl, called Amalia, w
22, 1822, Luise and Ra
separate and get a div
was not permitted to r
she became his commo
While his personal l
was increasingly succe
sionally directed at th
execution of his tasks
other long-term contr
the plays of the Old Vi
Vienna, at the theatei
Emperor attended one
1823. His Highness se
so well that he came t
städter Theater. Even
now and then overco
Some observers thougl
Only among a very sm
secure and at peace wii
Not satisfied with tl
appeared, or which he

Luise Gleich, who performed alongside of him as Evakathel. She was later to become Raimund's ill-fated wife. The success of this appearance paved the way for further invitations in 1816 and 1817, and an eventual long-term contract.

At the Josefstädter Theater, Josef Alois Gleich was the artistic director and resident playwright, who saw Raimund's great potential as a comedian. This was still contrary to Raimund's own appraisal of himself, for he persisted in thinking of himself as an actor of tragedies. At Gleich's recommendation, Raimund got to play the part of the comical character Kratzerl in *Die Musikanten am Hohenmarkt*. Raimund's portrayal of Adam Kratzerl made him instantly famous in Vienna. This part not only drew upon his acting ability, but also showed that he could sing, dance, and strum the violin. Gleich wanted to repeat this success by writing several sequels to *Die Musikanten am Hohenmarkt*. These included *Der Pudel des Herrn Kratzerl* (*Kratzerl's Poodle*) which had a well-trained poodle appear on stage, *Herr Kratzerl und seine Familie* (*Mister Kratzerl and his Family*), and finally *Adam Kratzerl als Dorfrichter* (*Adam Kratzerl as Village Judge*). The actor-director Ferdinand Rosenau at the Josefstädter Theater was moved to compose a parody of the Kratzerl cycle, which he entitled *Der Esel als Liebhaber* (*The Donkey as Lover*).

Though engaged as a permanent member of the Josefstädter Theater ensemble between 1814 and 1817, Raimund frequently accepted invitations for guest appearances from other theaters in and around Vienna. Particularly during the summers he performed at the theaters in Hietzing, Baden, and Pressburg, the same theaters where Raimund had started his acting career. But now he was a famous actor and no director would have dared not to pay him for a performance.

The Josefstädter Theater was the meeting place for servants and counts alike. Foreigners going through Vienna were also always brought to this theater, for it was a lively place to spend an evening. Secretly Raimund still entertained the thought that he was born to be an actor of tragedies. Thus he was pleased when asked to appear in Kringsteiner's parody of Shakespeare's *Romeo and Juliet*. This was a *Quodlibet* or medley of popular selections

from that play. In
only Shakespeare'
also the works of (

In October of
ensemble to accep
poldstädter Theate
debut there on Oc
vogels Witwensta
Zeitschrift" of the
dience with the qu

Raimund had fa
eighteen year old
come to Raimund
play, and he is su
taken by Therese
quickly changed
habit of dating m
one day in May,
became so infuria
of temper cost hir
battery. It would
muted the senten
Leopoldstädter Tl
this incident, his
took Raimund's an

The leading cor
Schuster. At first
ally became his ri
themselves into th
The management
each one appear
pacity each time.
comedian. Raimu
wig Costenoble (
from Hamburg in
tist [9] and had acce
take Raimund ald
tenoble recorded
he considered Ra

for them. These inserts consisted, for the most part, of new scenes, poems, jokes, and acrobatics. Most of them have been lost to posterity. Disappointed in the plays of Gleich, Bäuerle, and Meisl, he took the advice of friends and began to write his own plays. Raimund, however, had his reservations about this new step: "Hab i so nit Feinde genue? Soll i ma die Dichter auch noch zu Feinden machen?" ("Haven't I got enough enemies as it is? Why should I now make the poets enemies as well?")

In that day it was customary for actors to produce their own benefit plays. Invitations to well-to-do patrons would be delivered in person. Thus Meisl was instructed to write a benefit play for Raimund. Since he never got beyond the first act, Raimund decided to finish the play himself. This is how his first play Der Barometermacher auf der Zauberinsel came into being. Raimund's enemies tried to dispute his authorship, which forced him to state publicly just how this play came about. Raimund had written for himself the part of the barometermaker Bartholomäus Quecksilber. Friedrich Josef Korntheuer played the part of King Tutu, and Johanna Huber appeared as Zoraide. The play was a big success, and royalties kept flowing in from performances of this play on Viennese stages and abroad.

At last Raimund could afford to buy a horse and carriage. This made it possible for him to take long rides into the forests or the countryside. He took short trips to Baden and Brühl, where he spent many an afternoon. Raimund very much needed those moments of tranquillity to regain his equilibrium when something had affected him adversely at work or at home. Now and then he would go to the Burgtheater or visit close friends, such as Josef Ritter von Franck or Freiherr von Dankelmann.

The triumph of his first play led Raimund to write a second benefit play for himself, Der Diamant des Zauberkönigs, which was first performed on December 17, 1824. The ensemble's leading actress, Therese Krones, played the part of Mariandel, Korntheuer appeared as Zauberkönig, and Raimund portrayed Florian Waschblau. Costenoble thought the performance was a hit, in spite of the couple in the audience that kept saying : "Mer san nur Korntheuers wegen ins Theater ganga." ("We've only come to the theater to see Korntheuer.") The premiere audience included Archduke Karl, his wife, Archduke Anton, and the Prince of Salerno, all of whom are said to have made complimentary remarks about the play. Shortly afterwards, this play was also given at Graz, Lemberg, Trieste, Berlin, and Hamburg. And only two decades later Hans Christian Andersen adapted it for the Danish stage. Theater critics were commenting on how much better Raimund's second play was than the first one.[12]

After a hectic Summer trip with actor Josef Schmidt to Salzburg, Raimund was ready to stage his third play, *Das Mädchen aus der Feenwelt oder Der Bauer als Millionär*. It was premiered on November 10, 1826, with Raimund in the role of Fortunatus Wurzel. Some critics have compared this play with Shakespeare's *A Midsummer Night's Dream*. It has set many attendence records both in Vienna and abroad. For the Josefstädter Theater, Ferdinand Occioni wrote a parody entitled *Kolombine aus der Feenwelt oder Der Bauer als Millionär* (*Kolombine from the Fairy World or The Peasant as Millionaire*). And the Mödling Theater staged a parody called *Das Fischweib als Millionärin* (*The Fisherman's Wife as Millionairess*).

Moisasurs Zauberfluch was Raimund's next play, with which he hoped to show his critics that he was well versed in symbolism and mythology. His audiences, however, did not understand the play. And even though it gave rise to such parodies as Meisl's *Moisasuras Hexenspruch* and Heinrich Börnstein's *Monsieur Asurs sauberer Fluch*, Raimund's original version never really appealed to the Viennese public.

The young Pole Rudolf Steinkeller acquired control of the Leopoldstädter Theater and appointed Raimund its artistic director. This new appointment became official on April 17, 1828. Raimund was very flattered by this honor, but could not as yet foresee the difficulties this change in management was due to produce.

Die gefesselte Phantasie, Raimund's next play, was also intended as a sophisticated form of entertainment for the Viennese public. But the Viennese were again baffled by Raimund's intentions, and the play was dropped after only fourteen performances. Its only saving grace seemed to be Raimund's depiction of the Viennese harpist Nachtigall. Embittered about the way his contemporary public misunderstood his intentions of raising the level of the Old Viennese Popular Theater tradition, Raimund had another fit of melancholy and acute depression. Insult was added to injury when some critics doubted his authorship of this play, since it deviated so much from his earlier ones.[13] Later audiences were more charitable toward it. When the Raimundtheater opened in 1893, *Die gefesselte Phantasie* was the first play performed there.

More and more differences of opinion regarding the operation of the Leopoldstädter Theater arose between Raimund and Steinkeller. Steinkeller was highly arrogant and had no previous theatrical experience. He fired actors for alleged insubordination and failed to notify Raimund of such actions. This infuriated Raimund, who took extended journeys, from which he returned with a new play *Der Alpenkönig und der Menschenfeind*. This play was first performed on October 17, 1828, with Raimund in the role of the misanthrope Herr von Rappelkopf, and turned out to be a smashing hit. Erich Schmidt has called this play one of the most ingenious comedies of world literature.[14] The song "So leb' denn wohl, du stilles Haus" ("Farewell, you quiet home, we now must go") became an instantaneous hit, which developed into a folk song. Upon Grillparzer's suggestion, Raimund considered writing a sequel to this play, which was to be called *Eine Nacht am Himalaja* (*A Night in the Himalayas*). This project, however, was abandoned in a fragmentary state. In the meantime, *Der Alpenkönig und der Menschenfeind* was given abroad, where it was received with the same success as at home. Goethe had a favorable impression of this play. In 1831 the *Adelphi Theater* in London produced an adaptation by John Baldwin Buckstone entitled *King of the Alps and Misanthrope*. A critic in one of the English newspapers called Raimund's play one of the most original of that age.[15]

Raimund's next play, *Die unheilbringende Krone*, which was first performed on December 4, 1829, was misunderstood by the audiences. Raimund had labored hard to produce Alexandrine rhymes, with the end result that his public thought he was writing for the Burgtheater rather than the Old Viennese Popular Theater. Such erudite innovations made absolutely no impression upon it. The Theater an der Wien produced a parody entitled *Die goldpapierne Zauberkrone oder Nichts ist unmöglich*, which fared no better than the original play.

Under Steinkeller's management the Leopoldstädter Theater was slowly falling apart. A number of actors had been let go, and some of the stars, including Ignaz Schuster, Friedrich Korntheuer, Therese Krones, and Raimund himself were leaving. Raimund enjoyed his new freedom after August 1, 1830, when his contract expired. From now on, he wanted to perform at his own discretion and on his conditions. His fees became larger than ever before; however, no theater hesitated to pay them. And there were always more invitations that Raimund could possibly accept.

III *Search for Wider Horizons: 1830–1836*

Before his arrival at the Leopoldstädter Theater in 1817, Raimund had primarily played roles that others had developed before him in the traditional Old Viennese Popular Theater. The actors from whom he learned the most in his early career were Ferdinand Oschsenheimer, Anton Hasenhut, Anton Baumann, Tobias Kornhäusel, and Ignaz Schuster. In due course of time, Raimund surpassed them all in terms of versatility and popularity.

During his engagement at the Leopoldstädter Theater, he performed in plays that were either especially written for him, or that contained roles suited to his personality and talents. The Viennese audiences particularly liked to see him in those roles that required him to change into several different characters during one single performance, as in Meisl's *Das Gespenst auf der Bastei* and Gleich's *Der Eheteufel auf Reisen*. In the latter play Raimund danced and sang, and the public really loved it.

Between the appearance of his first play in 1823 and his departure from the Leopoldstädter Theater in 1830, Raimund preferred to appear in his own plays, which he had composed especially for himself. His roles included the barometermaker Quecksilber in *Der Barometermacher auf der Zauberinsel*, the servant Florian Waschblau in *Der Diamant des Geisterkönigs*, the harpist Nachtigall in *Die gefesselte Phantasie*, the village tailor Zitternadel in *Die unheilbringende Zauberkrone*, the farmer Gluthahn in *Moisasurs Zauberfluch*, the rich landlord Herr von Rappelkopf in *Der Alpenkönig und der Menschenfeind*, the farmer-millionaire Fortunatus Wurzel in *Der Bauer als Millionär*, and the loyal servant Valentin in his most popular play, *Der Verschwender*.

Between October, 1830, and January, 1831, Raimund made guest appearances at the Theater an der Wien, predominantly in his own plays, but also in such favorites of his, composed by other playwrights, as *Der Eheteufel auf Reisen, Der verzauberte Prinz, Das Gespenst auf der Bastei,* and *Die Fee aus Frankreich.* In February, 1831, he accepted an invitation to perform in Munich, primarily in his own plays. In Munich he struck up a friendship with the novelist Karl Spindler, whom he visited on subsequent trips to that city. Raimund preferred to spend the summers in or around Vienna. In the autumn of 1831, he travelled to Hamburg, but did not stay there for the full engagement because of an outbreak of cholera. November and December were spent in Munich, where he made a number of celebrated appearances at the Hoftheater. Upon the advice of a lawyer, he made his last will and testament, leaving everything to his common-law wife Toni.

The early part of 1832 was a miserable period for Raimund. He was very depressed and did not want to see anyone. These spells lasted for several months. Invitations from Berlin beckoned, and Raimund accepted. There he attempted to use High German instead of Viennese dialect, which confused his audiences. But once they understood his good intentions, they accepted them in good faith. Offered the management of the Königsstädtisches Theater in Berlin, he did not feel ready to take on this responsibility and graciously declined the offer. In September of the same year, he appeared in Hamburg.

On his return to Vienna, Raimund fell ill again. When he recovered, he appeared at the Josefstädter Theater and the Leopoldstädter Theater. By the autumn of 1833, he finished his next and last play, which he first called *Bilder aus dem Leben eines Verschwenders (Pictures from the Life of a Spendthrift)*. He later simplified the title to *Der Verschwender*. After no less than thirty-one rehearsals—an unheard-of number in those days—the play opened on February 20, 1834, at the Josefstädter Theater. Raimund portrayed the role of the loyal servant Valentin. This play became Raimund's all-time favorite with audiences in Austria and abroad. By the end of 1834, *Der Verschwender* had been performed more than one hundred times, quite a record in those days. Meisl wrote a parody entitled *Der Streitmacher,* which did not fare nearly as well as the original version.

With the great triumph he experienced with *Der Verschwender,* Raimund could sense that he was exhausted and that the

times were favoring the more aggressive style of Johann Nepomuk Nestroy. Nestroy's sarcastic wit began to supplant Raimund's gentle and naïve humor. Raimund's last appearance as an
actor took place on April 18, 1836, at the Stadttheater in Hamburg. He was a broken man, particularly when he noted that
Nestroy was beginning to take his place even in Germany.

Upon his return to Gutenstein, Raimund completely indulged
in his real and imagined illnesses. In this state of disparagement,
he and Toni went to the Shrine of Mariazell to pray for his health.
At their return, they were informed that their dog had bitten a
little girl, and since it was feared that the dog was infected with
rabies he had to be killed. Raimund was suddenly seized with the
apprehension that he himself might have contracted rabies. Both
headed for Vienna, where Raimund wished to consult a specialist.
A storm delayed them at an inn at Pottenstein, where he shot
himself the following morning. Doctors Johann Seibert and Josef
Wattmann-Marlcamy-Beaulieu along with his personal physician,
Dr. Rudolf von Lichtenfels, rushed from Vienna to Raimund's
bedside, but could not save him. He died on September 5, 1836.
Before he expired, he scribbled on a piece of paper: "Zu Gott
beten!" ("Let's pray to God!")

Although Raimund was dead, his acting tradition continued,
particularly with those actors who had known him in their lifetime, among them Ignaz Schuster, Johann Baptist Lang, Eduard
Weiss, Moritz Rott (Moritz Rosenberg), and Franz Wallner. Rott
was the first actor who dared to break away from acting patterns
established by Raimund. When succeeding generations performed Raimund's plays, they gave their own interpretations. The
great interpreters include Albin Swoboda, Ferdinand Schweig-
hofer, Ludwig Marinelli, Alexander Girardi, Rudolf Tyrolt, Willi
Thaller, Josef Bergauer, Ferdinand Maierhofer, Hermann Wawra,
Hermann Thimig, and the bothers Paul and Attila Hörbiger.

CHAPTER 3

Traditional Magic Parodies

RAIMUND did not leave completely authentic texts of his works. Deposited in the Austrian National Library are a number of variant manuscript versions of each of his works. Being very much attuned to the moods of the theater audiences, he made changes in his plays, which corresponded to the circumstances under which they were given. Since these variant manuscripts were not published in Raimund's life time, Eduard and Margarete Castle studied all available manuscripts and reconstructed the most representative version of each work in an effort to establish a definitive version.[1] Into these representative versions was introduced a normalization of spelling and punctuation which did the spirit and intentions of the author no harm. Different editors and compilers have drawn on different manuscripts for their sources.[2] The generally accepted standard edition, now out of print, is the "Historisch-kritische Säkularausgabe" of Raimund's works, edited by Fritz Brukner and Eduard Castle, in collaboration with Margarete Castle, Franz Hadamowsky, and Alfred Orel. Friedrich Schreyvogl's edition (Munich, 1960) of Raimund's works is based upon the text of this definitive edition. It contains all the basic texts, but omits letter's, reviews, and other important material contained in the out-of-print edition. Some of this material has recently been reproduced by Gustav Pichler in *Der unbekannte Raimund* (Vienna, 1962).

Raimund's plays are in either two or three acts, and his division of scenes is based on specific entrances and exits. He uses a combination of standard High German and phrases taken from the Viennese dialect, both of which were well understood then, as they are now, by speakers of the German language. Raimund chose his words very carefully and was infuriated if an actor forgot a word or placed the wrong accent on it. Even the well-seasoned actor Korntheuer received a tongue-lashing after a performance in which he had left out one word that he considered unimportant. To Raimund every single word, particularly as it concerned his own plays, was very important. As a writer and director of his own plays, he was a stickler for perfection and scheduled many more rehearsals than his colleagues thought necessary. Such rehearsals were costly, for they tied up not only the actors but also the many technicians required for the operation of the elaborate stage machinery.

I *The Barometermaker on the Magic Isle*

On several occasions Raimund wrote to Toni how dissatisfied he was with some of Gleich's and Meisl's plays that had been commissioned for production. He thought that some of them were poorly written and altogether lacking in ennobling features. He also objected to the slap-stick form of humor contained in them. After he had rewritten Meisl's *Das Gespenst auf der Bastei,* it was extremely well received by the public.

Christoph Martin Wieland's collection of fairy tales, *Dschinnistan oder Auserlesene Feen- und Geistermärchen,*[3] published in 1810, contained Friedrich Hildebrand von Einsiedel's fairy tale "Die Prinzessin mit der langen Nase" ("The Princess with the Long Nose"). Raimund commissioned Meisl to write a parody of this tale as a benefit play for him.

As Meisl never got beyond the first act, Raimund decided to rework that act and finish the play himself. The text was written down between mid-October and late November, 1823. When the play was completed, Raimund called it *Der Barometermacher auf der Zauberinsel.* The first performance took place on December 18, 1823, at the Leopoldstädter Theater, with Raimund in the role of Bartholomäus Quecksilber, Korntheuer as King Tutu, Johanna Huber as King Tutu's daughter Zoraide, and Miss Kupfer as Zoraide's chamber maid Linda. In later performances, Therese Krones made a name for herself by playing the part of the vivacious Linda. The play was a hit. Only one note of discord marred the event: rumor had it that the play was really written by Meisl. And since Meisl never commented on the matter, it was assumed that he was the author of this play. Raimund was indignant and placed an announcement in the papers explaining in some detail how the play came about.

The catchy music for this play was composed by Wenzel Müller (1767–1835), a long-time conductor and musical composer at the Leopoldstädter Theater. The fairytale was very popular with the Viennese audiences, for it consituted one of the most frequently performed genres of the Old Viennese Popular Theater. This being his first play, Raimund did not deviate too far from his source. He followed in the footsteps of his predecessors Meisl, Gleich, and Bäuerle. A thematic comparison between Einsiedel's fairytale "Die Prinzessin mit der langen Nase" and Raimund's *Der Barometermacher auf der Zauberinsel* will show how closely Raimund stuck to his source:

Prinzessin mit der langen Nase:

1. The Prince receives a magic box, which he considers an unworthy gift.

2. Instructions are found, indicating the extent of the magic powers of the objects in the box.
3. The Prince makes a grand entrance into the capital.
4. Princess Zenomide permits the Prince to woo her, if he tells her all about himself.

5. Zenomide snatches the magic objects from the Prince.
6. With his magic horn, the Prince summons an army to his aid.
7. Zenomide and her parents are taken prisoner.
8. Zenomide returns the magic objects to the Prince.
9. The army is dismissed, and Zenomide and the Prince are reconciled.

Barometermacher auf der Zauberinsel:

1. The barometermaker is given some magic implements, and wonders if someone is making a fool out of him.
2. Lidi explains how the magic implements work.

3. Reports circulate regarding the arrival of the barometermaker.
4. Princess Zoraide lets the barometermaker vie for her, if he divulges the secret concerning those magic implements.
5. Zoraide takes the magic wand from the barometermaker.
6. With his magic horn, the barometermaker brings an army to his side.
7. Zoraide and her father Tutu are incarcerated.
8. Zoraide returns the magic wand to the barometermaker.
9. After the army's dimissal, Zoraide feigns a reconciliation.

10. Zenomide extracts from the Prince information on how to use the magic horn, and then arrests him with an instantly contrived army.

11. As the Prince tries to use his magic belt against Zenomide, she snatches it from him and escapes.

12. The Prince escapes and attempts suicide, but in falling is caught by a fig tree. As he eats the figs, his nose becomes abnormally large. A drink from a magic well restores the nose to normal size.

13. The Prince hits upon the idea of selling the magic figs to Zenomide and her mother, whose noses quickly grow abnormally large.

14. Local doctors are unable to cure them. The Prince, disguised as an Egyptian physician, cures the mother, in return for which he receives the magic objects.

15. The Prince steps out of his disguise, snatches his magic objects, and leaves Zenomide with her long nose intact.

10. After prying from him the secret of the magic horn, Zoraide has the barometermaker arrested by an army of Amazons.

11. When the barometermaker attempts to use his magic belt against Zoraide, she takes it from him at knifepoint.

12. The barometermaker escapes and eats a fig, which gives him an abnormally large nose. A drink from a certain well restores the nose to normal size.

13. The barometermaker sees to it that the magic figs are delivered to King Tutu and Zoraide, whose noses suddenly grow out of all proportion.

14. As none of the house physicians can cure the affliction, the barometermaker appears disguised as an Egyptian physician, heals Tutu's nose and takes possession of the magic implements.

15. The barometermaker takes his magic implements and leaves Zoraide sporting an abnormally long nose.

Raimund followed the action of his source quite closely. He changed its locale from the fairytale world to his beloved Vienna. And there are some characters not originally contained in the fairytale, such as Zoraide's chambermaid Linda, King Tutu's valet Hassar, the nymph Lidi, and the forest dweller Zadi. All these new characters were drawn from the Viennese milieu. Their traits were rather weakly developed and their personalities do not exhibit very much individuality. By writing a parody of a fary-tale Raimund stuck very closely to the accepted form of the traditional Old Viennese Popular Theater, which was the regular fare at the suburban theaters.

The hero of this parody is the Viennese barometermaker Bartholomäus Quecksilber, who fails in his profession at home but succeeds resoundingly abroad. Quecksilber is a relative of the comical characters Kratzerl, Staberl, Kasper, and the rest. The chambermaid Linda slightly resembles the Columbine of the *Commedia dell'Arte*. Quecksilber also shows some kinship with Arlecchino, as he always knows how to say the right thing at the right time. What particularly amused the Viennese audiences was the fact that although Quecksilber travels to distant lands, he eventually comes back to dear old Vienna, which is after all the best of all possible places.

Character development goes much farther than was the case in the fairytale. All Raimund had to do was to observe his environment, which offered enough interesting personalities he could draw on for the inhabitants of his fairyland. Princess Zoraide resembles Luise Gleich. Both were exceedingly beautiful; however, the better one got to know them, the uglier they seemed. In contrast to Zoraide, there appears the bright-eyed, rosy-cheeked chambermaid Linda, who didn't have a single streak of meanness. Linda's naïve femininity may owe something to Toni Wagner.

Raimund must have drawn upon his own personality for some of the character traits found in the barometermaker. Both were naïve at first, but eventually learned how to handle Zoraide's and Luise's cunning wiles. At first baffled by capricious outbursts, both Raimund and the barometermaker eventually learn how to make the most of their situation. Although Raimund was not quite as successful in real life as the barometermaker is in his play, he could at least dream that some sort of justice existed in the magic world of a fairytale parody, if it did not exist in real life.

The basic conflict in this play is that between the mundane barometermaker and the cunning Princess Zoraide. From beginning to end, Quecksilber and Zoraide match wits. Each is trying to gain the upper hand. Imaginary magic powers enhance the interest in this conflict. The worlds of reality and illusion exist side by side, as though this were the most natural state of affairs. The sphere of the imagination is not something tucked away in the inner recesses of the mind; it is as much a part of life as the world of reality.

[64]

King Tutu, who looks like a typical Viennese, is still a character from the fairytale world. However, he was sufficiently well developed for some critics to have noticed a resemblance to Austria's reigning Emperor.[4] Francis I may or may not have recognized himself in King Tutu, but the Austrian audiences must have smiled at King Tutu's personality that was rampant with inertia, for it looked like a very familiar figure at the Imperial Court in Vienna.

The fig magic in this play was undoubtedly taken from the Baroque Court Opera, where it appeared, as well as from fairytales in which it was a favorite device. The Fortunatus Chap Book probably served as the source of the story of the magic objects used in both the fairy tale and Raimund's parody. Fortunatus, who appeared as the hero of a popular chivalric novel, also inspired Grillparzer, who planned to write a play, which he was going to call *Fortunats Wunschhütlein*.

Although a representative of the fairyland, Rosalinde strikes one as a typically Viennese girl in her behaviour and outlook on life. She even comes equipped with a feminine intuition, which Raimund calls in her case the "Lexikon der Menschheit" ("Dictionary of Humanity"), which she faithfully consults when in doubt. This intuition comes in very handy when the Viennese barometermaker appears and everyone is wondering who he might be. Rosalinde knows it right away.

Raimund's prevailing point of view throughout the play is positive and humane, and it persists even in moments of misfortune and despair. This is not only a parody of the fairy tale "Die Prinzessin mit der langen Nase", but also of the Viennese way of life, which has been superimposed upon the action of the fairy tale. By parodying the characters in the play, Raimund pokes fun at the same time at certain Viennese foibles and impossible customs. Generally the Viennese way of life is treated as though it were the best of all possible worlds.

Transitions from the world of reality to that of illusion were characterized by musical interludes and colorful fireworks, making them more palatable to the mind of the spectator. The chorus was also an integral part of the action of the play, as it moved into the spotlight to comment on the situations in the play, not dissimilar to the chorus of ancient Greek tragedy. This chorus, however, was typically Viennese and was not averse to singing and dancing merrily.

Der Barometermacher auf der Zauberinsel is also a vehicle of Raimund's own notion of justice. There is a self-sufficient sense of justice which requires that such asocial characters as Zoraide must be punished, and that such lovable people as Quecksilber should be rewarded. This abstract sense of justice greatly appealed to the Viennese and other audiences, for it suggests that justice is possible, if only in our imagination.

II *The Diamond of the Spirit King*

Encouraged by the success of *Der Barometermacher auf der Zauberinsel*, Raimund was confident enough to write a second play. In his autobiography,[5] he mentions that he attributed at least part of the triumph of his first play to his choice of a fairytale motif. This led him to look for another appropriate fairytale motif in the *Arabian Nights*. The two fairytales that provided him with the subject of *Der Diamant des Geisterkönigs* were "Die Geschichte des Prinzen Zein Alasnan und des Königs der Genien" ("Story of Prince Zein Alasnan and the King of Genies") and "Die Geschichte der beiden Schwestern, die ihre jüngste Schwester beneiden" ("Story of Two Sisters, Who Envy their Youngest Sister")[6] A third possible source that has been suggested is "Die drei ausgesetzten Königskinder" ("Three Abandoned Princes").[7] Albert Ludwig Grimm's translation of this fairytale was published by the Hirschfeld Publishing House in Vienna in 1824.[8] However, since the book was intended for children, many "objectionable" passages had been omitted. It was very difficult for Raimund to narrow down the sources he preferred, for once he had started reading *The Arabian Nights* he could not put the book down.

At first Raimund was going to call his new play "Der Zauberschatz" (The Magic Treasure"), but later he changed the title to *Der Diamant des Geisterkönigs*. The plot concerns the story of Eduard, son of the magician Zephises, who is to inherit great wealth after his father's death. The allegorical figure of Hope instructs Eduard on how to go about finding that promised wealth. He finds a hall which contains six mythological figures perched on pedestals. A seventh pedestal has its figure missing, but contains instructions and conditions with the help of which this figure can be claimed. The aid of the spirit king Longimanus must be sought. Eduard and his loyal servant Florian Waschblau set out to locate the spirit king and the diamond figure. On their journey to the spirit king, they are tested on their ability to follow instructions. When Florian imagines that he sees the likeness of his girl friend Mariandel, he disobeys instuctions and turns around to have another look at the apparition, and is changed into a poodle until the spirit king restores his human form. The conditions of acquiring that diamond statue require the location of a girl that has never lied. Florian was to serve as the human lie detector. If the girl they encountered had lied before, Florian would feel pain all over his body. Eduard's and Florian's search brings them to the "Country of Truth," where they are received by King Veritatius and his daughter Modestina. There they find Amine, the girl who has never lied, however, she is about to be sentenced to death for always telling the truth. On the trip back to the spirit king, Eduard falls desperately in love with Amine. With heavy heart he surrenders her to the king, and heads for home, where he is supposed to find the diamond statue on the seventh pedestal. When he arrives, he finds Amine on the seventh pedestal, and his happiness knows no bounds. Florian is also reunited with his beloved Mariandel.

Raimund was more original in his second play, and deviated more freely from his sources. Some changes had to be made in order to anticipate possible objections from the censors. In the original fairytale, the girl to be found was to be a virgin. And the search was to be undertaken with the help of a magic mirror. Making Florian into a human lie detector was Raimund's way of bringing the action closer to the human level of experience. Following Raimund's own conviction that a truthful girl is hard to find, Florian must skip and hobble in great pain around the stage before Amine is found. The audiences derived vicarious pleasure from Florian's protestations of pain, as they had earlier from the beatings of Kasperl, Thaddädl, and Hanswurst.

Der Diamant des Geisterkönigs was produced on December 17, 1824, at the Leopoldstädter Theater. Raimund played the role of the servant Florian Waschblau, Korntheuer the spirit king Longimanus, Landner the spirit king's valet Pamphilius, Krones Mariandel, and Schaffer Eduard. The allegorical figure of Hope was portrayed by Katharina Ennöckl. Josef Drechsler (1782–1852), who was active as a conductor and resident composer at the Leopoldstädter Theater since 1807, composed the music. Before his collaboration with Raimund he had written the music to many of Hensler's plays. Intended as a benefit play for Raimund, this work received greater acclaim than his first one.

It was customary in the tradition of the Old Viennese Popular Theater to depict women as fickle, loquacious, nagging, and predisposed to intrigue. Raimund disregards this tradition in introducing the kitchen maid Mariandel, whose warmth and naïveté, written into the part, quickly endeared her to the public. The traditional way of depicting men servants was to make them appear dishonest and unreliable. There, too, Raimund deviates from the norm by making Florian Waschblau loyal and dependable.

Two of the factors contributing to the popularity of this play were the complicated mechanical stage devices and the magnificent scenery required for its production. This intricate stage apparatus was very costly and required a large crew of maintenance men and technicians.

The character development shows more depth than was the case in Raimund's first play. In creating the vivacious figure of Mariandel, Raimund may have thought of his beloved, Toni. Therese Krones was particularly well suited for the interpretation of this role. Raimund's relationship with Toni was somewhat similar to that between Florian and Mariandel. Both couples loved, quarreled, and were reconciled. And jealousy often entered the picture.

To show that the four seasons in this play come from Vienna, Raimund has them speak in the Viennese dialect. The allegorical figure of Hope also shows typically Viennese traits. She feels that her existence is intended not only for the benefit of Eduard but for the world at large. The fire ghost shows traits of some overzealous Viennese, as the spirit king's valet, Pamphilius, depicts another character type, that of a person who never does anything right but is glib enough to say the right thing at the right time. The play presents these and other character types taken from the Viennese milieu.

Raimund's reaction to the conformity and the pusillanimous attitude found in the Biedermeier Period, is shown in the scenes (II, 15–16) that concern life in the "Country of Truth." There we encounter the girl Amine, whose greatest crime is that she never tells a lie. In that mythical country, everyone is free to tell the truth; however, if the truth concerns some cherished institution like King Veritatius, it is better left unsaid, unless it is highly complimentary. It is customary that when the king is happy, then the whole country is happy, too; and when the king is sad, the whole country shares that mood. When Amine refuses to pretend to be what she is not, she is quickly branded a traitor deserving punishment. The only thing that saves her is the appearance of the foreigners Eduard and Florian, who are seeking a girl that has never lied.

One of the heroes of this play is Eduard, the son of the magician Zephises. Some critics have seen him as a spoiled child from the upper classes, who is ill prepared to take on the tasks of life without the help of a servant like Florian. Others, like Heinz Kindermann,[9] regard him as an elevated kind of human being, on the order of those developed by Jean Paul. To Kindermann, Eduard appears less concerned with material rewards than with metaphysical considerations. In the struggle between duty and love, he chooses duty. Eduard is a forerunner of Julius Flottwell in Raimund's later play, *Der Verschwender*.

Eduard's steady and loyal companion throughout this play is the servant Florian Waschblau, who reminds one of Shakespeare's wise fools. Like the fool in *King Lear*, who could tell which of the king's daughters intrigued against him, Florian's extrasensory powers can tell him whether a girl he encounters has ever lied. Florian is rightly indignant when he enters the "Country of Truth," and his frankness is mistaken for absentmindedness: "What? They want to throw me into that fool's prison, and I'm smarter than all of them put together." (II, 14)

Although there appears to be a relationship between Florian Waschblau and the barometermaker Bartholomäus Quecksilber in Raimund's first play, and indirectly with the comical figures of Kratzerl, Kasperl, and Thaddädl, Florian is infinitely more resourceful than his predecessors. Some critics have seen a relationship between Florian and Tamino in *Die Zauberflöte*. A kinship can also be established with the modern non-hero, who shows seeds of his origin in a character like Florian. However, life was anything but absurd to Florian, for he firmly believed that he lived in the best of all possible worlds.

The kitchen maid Mariandel resembles Linda in Raimund's first play. Both are contented and happy and accept life and all it has to offer in a naïve way. They hail from the Viennese suburbs, where the lower middle classes lived. Mariandel is somewhat more developed and outspoken than Linda. Her sense of humor and love of life is contagious.

The Italian dramatist Carolo Gozzi had also adapted the same fairytale from *The Arabian Nights* and made it into a play of his own. Raimund claimed that he had never seen Gozzi's version until he had finished his own.[10] Gozzi deviated much less from the original than Raimund. The original version laid greater stress upon the activities of the spirit king. The finding of a pure maiden signified there a change of fortune, not only for the king, but also for his people. The principal theme of the original and of Gozzi's version is self-improvement, while Raimund emphasized the triumph of virtue and duty, which is also the triumph of love and beauty.

Der Diamant des Geisterkönigs was a hit not only in Vienna and other parts of Austria, but also in Trieste, Prague, Berlin, and Hamburg. In 1849, the Danish poet Hans Christian Andersen adapted this play for the Danish stage and called it *Meer end Perler og Gold* (*More Pearls than Gold*).[11] Andersen's version was produced on October 3, 1849, at the Casino Theater in Copenhagen. This was a popular theater, somewhat on the order of the suburban Old Viennese Popular Theater.

CHAPTER 4

Original Magic Extravaganzas

AFTER his last appearance in *Der Diamant des Geisterkönigs,* Raimund was totally exhausted and, upon the advice of his physician, Dr. Rudolf von Lichtenfels, he went on a vacation that lasted several months. On October 7, 1825, he returned to the stage and performed the part of the landlord in Korntheuer's *Alle sind verheiratet (Everyone is Married).* A number of intimate friends presented him with a commemorative medal, which contained his portrait and the inscription: "From his admirers on the eve of his recovery."

When he was not active in the theater, he spent his time at the "Silbernes Kaffeehaus" or at the "Kaffeehaus zum Stern." There he chatted with Franz Grillparzer, Eduard von Bauernfeld, Count Anton von Auersperg, Niembsch von Strehlenau, who was better known as Nikolaus Lenau, Franz von Schober, Ernst von Feuchtersleben, and Theodor Georg von Karajan. This was a group of intellectuals who sought each other's company. It was within this group that a mutual admiration between Raimund and Grillparzer developed. Both professed a deep affection for Vienna and owed their initial development as playwrights to the Old Viennese Popular Theater tradition.

The success of his first two plays led Raimund to believe that he could do better than just follow the prevailing taste of the Old Viennese Popular Theater. He wanted to raise the literary level of his own plays. Visits to the Burgtheater and long discussions with Grillparzer convinced him that he was ready to attempt a synthesis of the Old Viennese Popular Theater with the classical drama. To show his independence of his predecessors, Raimund called each of his subsequent plays "original" and set out to create magic extravaganzas which he secretly hoped would take their place next to the dramatic masterpieces of Grillparzer, Shakespeare, and the Greek tragedies.

I *The Peasant as Millionaire*

The plans for his next play began to materialize in the autumn of 1825, and came to fruition by the spring of 1826. Josef Edler von Manquet, an administrator of the Leopoldstädter Theater, read Raimund's manuscript of *Das Mädchen aus der Feenwelt oder Der Bauer als Millionär*, liked it, and accepted it for production. Wishing to write something that was superior to what he had written before, Raimund reworked this manuscript several times before he felt that it was ready for production.[1] The play was given for the first time on November 10, 1826. Raimund collaborated with Josef Drechsler (1782–1852) on the musical score, which included a number of songs, like "Brüderlein fein" and the "Aschenlied," which became popular folksongs overnight.

The plot concerns Lacrimosa, the fairy, who marries a mortal man by whom she has a baby girl: "Das Mädchen aus der Feenwelt" ("The girl from the Fairyland"). Lacrimosa wants her daughter to marry none other than the Prince of Fairies. Outraged by this presumption, the Queen of Fairies deprives Lacrimosa of her magic powers and decrees that her daughter is to marry a virtuous young man before she turns eighteen. The peasant Fortunatus Wurzel is entrusted with Lacrimosa's daughter and instructed to marry her off in the manner prescribed. In the meantime she is to be educated in the virtues of simplicity and honesty. The allegorical figure of Envy proceeds to corrupt Wurzel by showering him with undeserved wealth. Wurzel becomes a millionaire and insists that Lacrimosa's daughter Lottchen should marry a wealthy man rather than the poor fisherman Karl Schilf. To get out of this predicament, Lacrimosa calls all the ghosts and magicians to her aid. Unconvinced, the millionaire Wurzel vows not to change his mind until he is overcome by old age. Wurzel's youth departs prematurely, he grows old suddenly, and Lottchen and Karl get married. Wurzel recognizes that wealth has only corrupted him, gives it up and reverts to his peasant state, in which he was a happy man.

At the premiere of this play, Raimund appeared as the peasant-millionaire Fortunatus Wurzel, a role he had written for himself, and which allowed him again to show his versatility in changing from a middle-aged man into an old man. Korntheuer appeared as the Hungarian magician Bustorius, and Therese Krones gave an unforgettable performance as the allegorical figure of Youth. Therese Krones had become a symbol of femininity to many Viennese men.

Though Rudolf Prisching suggests that this play is based on Carl Meisl's *Der lustige Fritz*, in which Raimund had played the leading role on several occasions, he offers little actual evidence to substantiate his assertion.[2] The only circumstantial relationship concerns the general similarity between the two protagonists, who experience major changes in their lives. Both plays also contain ghosts and allegorical figures. A more valid comparison might be made with Grillparzer's *Der Traum ein Leben*, which was written eight years later. When Raimund witnessed the premiere of this play, he claimed to have expressed essentially the same idea, with a different emphasis, in his own *Der Bauer als Millionär*.

Wealth as a corruptor of human beings had been depicted by Meisl, Gleich, and Bäuerle, but never quite as convincingly and with as much relevance to the lives of the contemporary Viennese. Raimund's use of magic characters in commenting on the need for social justice and modesty has given this play universal appeal. To underline his point of view, Raimund depicted Fortunatus Wurzel as a finer human being when he was a poor peasant than when a man of wealth. Wealth only corrupts Wurdel into egomania with a lack of compassion for his fellow human beings. As a millionaire, his major urge is to fill his stomach, and his second thought concerns the many flatterers and wheedlers who are gathered about him like parasites. Old and loyal friends who do not fit into this new decadent pattern are quickly disposed of. Wurzel would not mind a bit of education, but finds the process depressingly difficult. Instead, he acquires many boxes of books, which he dutifully inscribes with his full name, and then proceeds to use them as decorations. On one occasion, Wurzel naïvely approaches his physician with the request to get him some medicine that contains ingredients to enhance his intelligence. For a moment the physician hesitates, but then decides to take advantage of the gullibility of this *nouveau riche* and regularly supplies him with a potion for that purpose, charging an exorbitant fee. Wurzel's belief that

money can buy everything is so strong that he continues this practice as long as he has more money than he knows what to do with.

One of the most effective scenes of this play concerns Youth
taking leave of Wurzel. This event will have a special appeal for
people who take youth for granted until it leaves them. This sixth
scene in Act II of the play is worthy of reproduction:

YOUTH

Heaven greet you, brother, I hope you don't mind that I pay my
respects personally?

WURZEL

That's a fine looking fellow! Not dry behind the ears, and foolish as
can be. Never saw me in his life and right away it's "brother"!

YOUTH

Yes, brother, I've got a special matter to take up with you.

WURZEL

Well, brother, what can I do for you? (*To himself*) He wants money
for sure.

YOUTH

Yes—don't hold it against me, brother, but it's all over between us.
I've come to cancel our friendship.

WURZEL

Well, that's a fine thing, brother, we've just met, brother, and we're
supposed to be sore at each other already, brother—that's no way
to act.

YOUTH

Ha, ha! What are you thinking of, brother? You're all wrong. Our
friendship has to end just because we've known each other too long.
We came into the world together, don't you even remember *that* any
more?

WURZEL

Oh, sure, sure! I remember. In the afternoon, and it rained.

YOUTH

We went to school together, too. Don't you remember? We sat on the
same bench together.

[74]

WURZEL

That's right! We sat in the corner. (*To himself*) Don't know him at all.

YOUTH

Sure! They tried to make us learn something there.

WURZEL

Yeah, what a lot of foolery that was—but they didn't put that over on us. We sure were a couple of rascals. (*To himself*) Never saw him before in my life.

YOUTH

And when we were both twenty, we really tore up the town. Was that ever something, brother!

WURZEL

Yeah, what a laugh! (*To himself*) News to me!

YOUTH

And all those times we got drunk together, brother, what a mess!

WURZEL

Just awful, brother!

YOUTH

Yes, and what all we used to drink!

WURZEL

Sure, why, I bet we even drank wine once. What a sin!

YOUTH

Yes, and what a wine!

WURZEL

A Luttenberger.

YOUTH

And a Grinzinger.

WURZEL
(*To himself*)

All a big lie!

[75]

YOUTH

You dragged me around to every tavern, we were really plastered every day—a couple of real sots.

WURZEL
(*Aside*)

He must not be a complete stranger; he sure knows me. (*Aloud*) Brother, we'll do it all over again. Have a drink, brother!

YOUTH

No, brother! It's all over. Now you've got to turn respectable. You have to go to bed at seven o'clock, you mustn't get drunk any more —well, you'll find out all you have to do now from somebody else— he'll tell you soon enough.

WURZEL

Ah, what's all that? Not get drunk! Me not drunk? That's the noblest thing about me. I'm so healthy I can take on an army.

YOUTH

Yes, brother, now, as long as I'm with you. (*Strongly*) But as soon as I take a single step out of this room, you'll want to stop tempting fate.

WURZEL
(*Aside*)

Now I'm getting worried. This guy might put a hex on me! Some brotherhood!

YOUTH

So farewell, dear brother. Forgive me for the unhappiness I've caused you, my dear friend! I'm really a good fellow, I've stuck with you long enough. You were my closest friend, but now you're a dissolute sot, so good-bye, brother—don't be angry with me, and don't run me down when I'm gone.

Duet
YOUTH

Brother o' mine, brother o' mine,
Don't be angry, please don't pine!
Sunshine lasts you just a day,
Night must come and ever stay!
Brother o' mine, brother o' mine,
Don't be mad and pine.

[76]

WURZEL

Brother o' mine, brother o' mine,
Don't be childish, drink my wine!
Here's ten thousand thaler—see!
Ev'ry year you stay with me.

YOUTH

No, no, no, no,
Brother o' mine, brother o' mine,
You're not talking, just the wine;
Money's lord in ev'ry land,
Only Youth escapes its band!
So brother o' mine, brother o' mine,
Parting now is next in line!
Brother o' mine, brother o' mine,   )
Soon I'll say farewell.   )
                        WURZEL   )   BOTH
)
Brother o' mine, brother o' mine,   )
Please don't say farewell.   )
(*Youth and his company dance during the ritornello*)

YOUTH

Brother o' mine, brother o' mine,
In your face is anger's sign,
Hatred here will hold its sway,
After I have gone away.
Brother o' mine, brother o' mine,
Don't make hatred thine.

WURZEL

Brother o' mine, brother o' mine,
If you're such a rascal—fine!
If you won't stay a friend,
Devil take you, there's an end!

YOUTH

No, no, no, no,
Brother o' mine, brother o' mine,
Friendly parting's my design;
Think of me in later years,
Don't remember Youth with tears!
Brother o' mine, brother o' mine,
Here's my hand in thine!

BOTH

Brother o' mine, brother o' mine,
Here's my hand in thine!
(*They embrace. Youth dances out followed by his company.*) (II, 6)

And thus Youth departs and leaves Fortunatus Wurzel an old man. There is infinite pathos in Wurzel's aria. It contains the Christian ideal that man was dust, and no matter how much he wriggles and quivers, in the end he shall turn into dust again. In a conversation with the allegorical figure of Contentment, Wurzel admits to his youthful faults and sings an aria that has always touched the public wherever this play was given:

Aria

So many men you find,
From pride they're nearly blind,
Their clothes so fine to see,
But dumb as dumb can be,
Conceited as a pig,
Oh boy, they think they're big!
But once the fun's all through,
They'll all be ashmen too!
　　　Just ashes! Just ashes!

There goes a pretty maid,
All fine in lace and braid,
I take a closer look,
It's just some merchant's cook!
Just pack that frock away,
The kitchen's where you'll stay!
The world's a mixed-up case,
When cooks don't know their place!
　　　Just ashes! Just ashes!

But some things still I've seen,
And gold's not what I mean,
That do deserve respect,
That stand without defect.
Before good people here,
Before kind deeds and cheer,

Original Magic Extravaganzas

In faithful maiden's praise,
My hat I humbly raise.
    (*Removes his hat*)
    No ashes! No ashes! (III, 4)

Fortunatus Wurzel is the symbol of man, whose soul is torn between several alternative courses in life. He must make a choice between simplicity and luxury, between happiness and superficiality, and ultimately between the ideal and the real. Raimund saw these conflicts as elemental to the human condition. He strongly believed that happiness and truth flourish in conjunction with simplicity and modesty, rather than luxury and ostentatiousness. Raimund made Wurzel into the vehicle for his conviction that happiness in life was closely related to modesty and contentment. He saw the world composed of certain social strata which should not be altered, unless one wished to endanger man's physical and mental equilibrium. The danger of sudden changes was that they frequently led to decadence, human alienation, and even chaos.

Der Bauer als Millonär was a great hit. By 1827, it had been given over eighty times. In addition to its enthusiastic reception in Vienna and other parts of Austria, it was also given to full houses in Leipzig, Berlin, Hamburg, Pest, Prague, Brünn, Munich, Frankfurt on Main, and Dresden. Meisl wrote a parody entitled *Fee Sanftmut und Fee Gefallsucht (Fairy Gentleness and Fairy Coquetry)*, which was given as a benefit play for the actress Katharina Ennöckl at the Leopoldstädter Theater. Ignaz Schuster played the role of Fortunatus Wurzel. Another parody, *Kolombine aus der Feenwelt (Kolombine from the Fairy World)* by Ferdinand Occioni, was produced at the Josefstädter Theater. Even the Meidling Theater staged a parody, *Das Lerchenfelder Mädchen oder Das Fischweib als Millionärin (The Lerchenfeld Girl or The Fisherwoman as Millionairess)*.

II *Inhibited Imagination*

Die gefesselte Phantasie was completed in a mere three months. Although finished by September, 1826, the play did not reach the stage until January 8, 1828. The audiences received the play with mixed emotions. Two factions formed one believing that

[79]

Raimund was really attempting to write for the Burgtheater and should have his plays produced there; the other thinking that the playwright had introduced too many unfamiliar mythological and allegorical allusions unsuited to the Old Viennese Popular Theater tradition. The second faction was the larger one, and Raimund felt hurt by this reaction.

The setting for the *Die gefesselte Phantasie* is the world of antiquity. Hermione is the queen of the peninsula Flora, where the inhabitants devote their lives to creative writing under Apollo's divine protection. Amphio, son of King Athunt, who rules the neighboring kingdom, is in love with the queen. Hermione's land is ravaged by Vipria and Arrogantia, who represent evil and arrogance. The oracle proclaims that as soon as Hermione marries a poet, the land will be free from Vipria and Arrogantia, and peace, along with creative tranquillity, will again reign. Amphio, with the help of the allegorical figure of Imagination, becomes a master of the poetic arts in spite of the competition from the Viennese harpist Nachtigall and those evil sisters Vipria and Arrogantia. Queen Hermione marries Amphio, as Vipria and Arrogantia are banished, and *belles lettres* becomes again the favorite preoccupation of the residents of Flora.

In this play, Raimund portrayed the struggle between an ideal poetic world and a harsh world of reality. This ideal world was conceived in perfect order and justice, whereas the world of reality was imperfect and corrupt. Raimund's ideal poetic world was a creation of his own imagination, which he wished to bring into harmony with the world of reality. To render the contrast meaningful, Raimund opposed the ideal land of Flora and its inhabitants with that of the Viennese harpist Nachtigall and life in a suburban inn.

When this play opened at the Leopoldstädter Theater on January 8, 1828, it was not well received by the public, which simply did not understand it. It was not like what it had come to expect from the Old Viennese Popular Theater. Embittered by this reaction, Raimund decided that the poor reception was probably due to poor acting and changed his cast. However, this maneuver didn't affect the public's continued disapproval of the play at that time. It fared better in 1830 at the Theater an der Wien. On several occasions Nestroy himself appeared as the harpist Nachtigall. And

Original Magic Extravaganzas

when the Raimund Theater opened in 1893, it did so with *Die gefesselte Phantasie* under the direction of Adam Müller-Guttenbrunn. When this play was performed five years later at the Hoftheater at Karlsruhe under the direction of Eugen Kilian and Felix Mottl, Wenzel Müller's musical score was replaced by a piece by Franz Schubert. Schubert's musical score was also used when *Die gefesselte Phantasie* was given for the first time at the Burgtheater on September 12, 1936, under the direction of Herbert Waniek.[3]

Before and after Raimund's death, this play was much better received abroad than at home. Audiences in Munich, Hamburg, and Berlin showed great respect for it, particularly when Raimund himself appeared as Nachtigall. Berlin's "Vossische Zeitung" viewed with disfavor the unfriendly reception the work had received in Vienna.

Heinz Kindermann has been most appreciative of this work.[4] He regards Raimund as a musical poet, similar to Grillparzer, who imbues the plastic world of reality with an appropriate musical soul. The expression of this musical soul is closely akin to the ideal musical drama by Richard Wagner. It is a well-known fact that Wagner consulted *Die gefesselte Phantasie* during his composition of *Die Meistersinger von Nürnberg*.

The allegorical figure of Imagination represents Raimund's own liberation from the fetters of the Old Viennese Popular Theater tradition. This liberation took place with the help of such mentors as Shakespeare, Goethe, Schiller, Grillparzer, and Calderón. Between 1814 and 1832 Joseph Schreyvogl actively fostered the production of these world classics of drama at the Burgtheater, which Raimund frequented to supplement his theatrical education.

Flora's Queen Hermione shows a relationship to Lacrimosa in *Der Bauer als Millionär*. Both are in a quandary. Hermione's antagonists are the two evil sisters Vipria and Arrogantia; Lacrimosa's enemies are the allegorical figures of Envy and Hatred. Raimund makes sure, however, that in the end virtue triumphs. With the aid of the Imagination, Amphio not only liberates himself, but also Hermione. The harpist Nachtigall was a role Raimund had written for himself, and which represented an aspect of his own personality. Both had a volatile temper and suffered from the awareness that the world had not given them full recognition. Nachtigall was no safer from Vipria's and Arrogantia's plotting than Raimund from the wagging tongues of evil and arrogance that surrounded him from time to time.

Walter Erdmann has suggested a comparison between *Die gefesselte Phantasie* and Novalis' *Heinrich von Ofterdingen*.[5] He cites the fact that a curse of sorts enveloped both plots, and that a stranger was expected to arrive and restore order. In Novalis' story it was Eros; in the case of Raimund's play, Amphio. Vipria's and Arrogantia's chaining of the Imagination renders the poets incapable of writing poetry, just as the appearance of Night in Novalis' work produces similar effects upon the environment. Carrying the comparison beyond this basic similarity would be futile.

With his creation of the fool Muh in *Die gefesselte Phantasie*, Raimund introduced a character very similar to Shakespeare's fools. Erdmann suggests other similarities to the style and work of Shakespeare. There exists a particular affinity to *Timon of Athens* as far as style and ideology are concerned. Both plays show didactic tendencies. In each instance the author makes his comment about the villainy of human nature. The objections concerning the dramatic shortcomings of Raimund's play can also be applied to Shakespeare's *Timon of Athens*.

Among those critics who did not like this work of Raimund, Rudolf Fürst was the most outspoken.[6] He disliked *Die gefesselte Phantasie* because he thought he saw in it many irregularities of structure and plot, as well as certain touches of vulgarity. Hermione and Amphio appeared too weakly drawn, just as Amphio's prize poem seemed highly pedestrian. Nor did Fürst like Wenzel Müller's score. In the production at the Hoftheater in Karlsruhe, the director not only substituted Schubert's music for Müller's, but also replaced the prize poem which Amphio recites to win Hermione.[7] And finally, Fürst believed that the use of French Alexandrines did absolutely nothing to enhance the dramatic quality of *Die gefesselte Phantasie*.

III *Moisasur's Magic Curse*

Begun on May 19, *Moisasurs Zauberfluch* was finished by June 20, 1827. Most of the text was written down at Weidling am Bach, where Raimund spent the summer with Toni. When he could not reach an agreement with the management of the Leopoldstädter Theater regarding the royalties of this play, it was given on September 25 of the same year at the Theater an der Wien. This was the first time that Raimund did not appear in a role at the premiere of one of his own plays. Director Carl appeared as Gluthahn. Some have suggested the Alceste motif in Christoph Willibald Gluck's opera *Alceste* of 1767 as a possible basis for *Moisasurs Zauberfluch*. There seems to be as much evidence against this theory as there is for it.

The action takes place in fabled India. Alzinde, the virtuous wife of King Hoanghu, decides to destroy the temple of the evil demon Moisasur and erect, in its stead, a temple dedicated to Virtue. Moisasur avenges himself by turning every human being in the land into stone. This curse will be lifted only when Alzinde sheds tears of joy. On her journey, Alzinde encounters a ruthless farmer called Gluthahn and a poor but compassionate peasant couple, Hans and Mirzel, who live in the Alpine region of Austria. Hoanghu is so much in love with his wife that he offers half of his life for hers, which so touches her that she sheds tears of joy. Thus Moisasur's curse is broken, and Alzinde and Hoanghu return to their native land under the protection of their guardian angel Virtue.

Moisasurs Zauberfluch was written during the same tense emotional period of self-doubts and pessimism in Raimund's life, during which he also created *Die gefesselte Phantasie* and *Der Bauer als Millionär*. Each of these plays is divided into a stylized, idealized sphere of activity and a realistic one. On the one side there are demons and magic characters, on the other side a variety of human beings. Each of these two groups is further subdivided into those characters who support evil and those who support virtue. Of the human beings in this play, Gluthahn is by far the most despicable, whereas Hans and Mirzel are a couple representing kind and simple country folk. The tender care with which Raimund depicts them suggests that he had great admiration for this type, whom he met on occasion when he journeyed out of the city to escape the hypocrisies and intrigues that enveloped him at times.

The ideal world is located in the mysterious Orient. It was fashionable for the Romantics, particularly for Friedrich Schlegel, to seek wisdom and justice in the Orient.[8] Raimund and many of his contemporaries who were disgusted with the lack of justice, good taste, and high ideals in their part of the world, sought these qualities in the mysterious East through poetic imagination. And since the imagination cared little about facts, salvation was not far away.

Like Shakespeare, Raimund often used the device of contrast in his plays. Fabled India is contrasted with Alpine Europe, the vicious Gluthahn with the amiable couple Hans and Mirzel, the brutal demon Moisasur and the compassionate allegorical figure of Virtue, the impulsive Alzinde and her devoted husband King Hoanghu, and, more generally, the world of reality and the world of illusion.

Comparing Gluthahn and Moisasur with earlier incarnations of evil forces in Raimund's works, such as Envy and Hatred in *Der Bauer als Millionär*, or the evil ghosts and genii in *Der Diamant des Geisterkönigs* and *Der Barometermacher auf der Zauberinsel*, it becomes evident how much more destructive and devoid of humor Gluthahn and Moisasur are. This may in part represent Raimund's own conviction that the more famous he became, the more vicious were his enemies; and Gluthahn and Moisasur may well stand for some of his own foes. It is a known fact that Raimund drew upon people he knew for the characteristics of the heroes and villains of his plays.

Along with Bartholomäus Quecksilber and Florian Waschblau in Raimund's earlier works, Alzinde is employed to measure the degree of love, truth, and human compassion she encounters in the hearts of those she meets. Alzinde also determines the humaneness of those she sees. She is shocked beyond belief when she encounters the brutal Gluthahn. She repeatedly asks him: "Are you a human being? Do you have a heart in that chest?" Convinced of the basic goodness of man, Alzinde, like Raimund, maintains that those who have strayed from human compassion and nobility need only to consult the dictates of their heart and soul to return to that bond that unites all mankind.

Heinz Kindermann has noticed a number of parallels between Raimund's *Moisasurs Zauberfluch* and Goethe's *Faust II*.[9] Both plays took their bourgeois public by surprise, having been used to realistic and trivial plots, they were bewildered by such grand allegories and flights into ancient mythology. Both plays were parodied. One is particularly reminded of Friedrich Theodor

Vischer's witty parody *Faust, Dritter Teil,* which he published under the pseudonym Deutobold Symbolizetti Allegoriowitsch Mystifizinsky. Raimund's and Goethe's unconventional treatment of human relationships in their works contributed to the confusion with which the public received them. Kindermann placed Raimund's *Moisasurs Zauberfluch* within a line of works that emanates from the dance dramas of the Middle Ages and continues through the Baroque Theater, Goethe's *Faust II,* and Richard Wagner's musical drama, to the plays of our day.

Literary historians will record *Moisasurs Zauberfluch* as a precursor of the tragic and comic peasant dramas of Ludwig Anzengruber (1839–1889), Franz Kranewitter (1860–1938), and Karl Schönherr (1867–1943). Peasant dramas before Raimund depicted their heroes as simpletons or as noble savages. The peasant Gluthahn not only personifies evil and inhumanity, but also has a personality of his own within the context of Alpine peasantry. The line of character development from Gluthahn in *Moisasurs Zauberfluch* leads directly to Anzengruber's *Meineidbauer,* and *Der G'wissenswurm,* to Schönherr's *Der Judas von Tirol,* and Kranewitter's *Michel Gaissmayr.*

Moisasurs Zauberfluch had a mixed reception in the newspapers. It also gave rise to a number of parodies. On November 3, 1827, Meisl's *Moisasuras Hexenspruch* was performed at the Leopoldstädter Theater, where the management had balked at the high royalties Raimund demanded. Wenzel Müller composed the music to Meisl's parody. Karl Gladt's comparative study of Raimund's *Moisasurs Zauberfluch* and Meisl's *Moisasuras Hexenspruch oder Die Zerstörung des Kaffeetemples*[10] found Meisl's travesty neither original nor funny. There is room for disagreement with this study, particularly as it concerns the funny scene in which Meisl parodies Moisasur's Temple with his creation of a temple dedicated to the Goddess of Coffee. Comedian Ignaz Schuster portrayed Gluthahn, and Therese Krones appeared as Alzinde in this parody. Another parody by Friedrich Adami and Heinrich Börnstein[11] appeared at the *Josefstädter Theater.* It was called *Monsieur Asurs sauberer Fluch* (*Mr. Asur's Clean Curse*).

Moisasurs Zauberfluch was performed regularly at the Josefstädter Theater well into the middle of the nineteenth century. Memorable productions of this work took place in 1881 at the Gärtnerplatztheater in Munich, and in 1900 at the Kaiser Jubiläum's Theater in Vienna. The Viennese poet Herbert Johannes Holz wrote a radio play version of Raimund's original, which was published in 1958.[12] The play, which in Raimund's life time was thought by many to belong on the stage of the Burgtheater, was not performed there until May 12, 1960. The magnificent scenery was designed by Oskar Kokoschka.[13] This grand production, which was produced by Gustav Pichler, featured Heinz Moog as Moisasur, Aglaja Schmidt as Alzinde, and the celebrated Hermann Thimig as Gluthahn, under the direction of Max Mell and Rudolf Steinboeck.

IV   *The Fatal Crown*

Originally entitled "Die glühende Krone" (*The Glowing Crown*), Raimund eventually named this play *Die unheilbringende Krone oder König ohne Reich, Held ohne Mut, Schönheit ohne Jugend*.[14] Written slightly over a year after *Der Alpenkönig und der Menschenfeind*, it is treated in this chapter because of its close affinity to the other three plays discussed here. Composed between August 25 and October 2, 1829, *Die unheilbringende Krone* was first performed at the Leopoldstädter Theater on December 4, 1829. It was not well received by the public, even though Raimund himself appeared in the role of Simplizius Zitternadel, along with Josefine Planer as Lucina. The musical score was composed by Josef Drechsler, who had collaborated with Raimund in *Der Diamant des Geisterkönigs* and *Der Bauer als Millionär*. The audiences objected to Raimund's departure from the simple comical plots they had come to expect from the Old Viennese Popular Theater.

The plot deals with the life of Phalarius, a field marshal in the service of Kreon, King of Agrigent. Convinced that he deserves to be king because he saved the kingdom by his military exploits, Phalarius eventually accepts the "fatal crown" from Hades, king of the underworld. This crown is so powerful that everyone approaching it immediately succumbs to it. Phalarius becomes King of Agrigent as Kreon flees under the protection of his guardian spirit Lucina. To restore Kreon to his throne, Lucina gets Hades to agree to a wager, according to which she would furnish him with "a country without a crown, a hero without courage, and a youth without beauty" if he restores Kreon to the throne. To Hades' great surprise, Lucina wins her wager, and Kreon is restored to his throne with the aid of the three furies Tisiphone, Megäre, and Alecto.

Phalarius was Raimund's poetic depiction of Napoleon. Both Phalarius and Napoleon won their crowns through military exploits and lost them when they overextended themselves. Raimund may also have been inspired by Gleich's *Der Hölle Zaubergaben* (*Hell's Magic Gifts*) and *Die bezauberte Leier* (*The Magic Lyre*). The strongest impulse seems to have come from Shakespeare's *Macbeth*. Like *Macbeth*, Raimund's play suffers from certain inconsistencies in the plot. The plot in each instance is partly historical, partly based on the literary tradition of the day, and partly invented. Both playwrights have taken liberties with their historical sources, and freely move the action of their plays between the world of reality and the world of magic. The conceptual unity of these plays is established by the notion that nobility and virtue must triumph over excessive ambition. And both Macbeth and Phalarius remain remorseless villains unto their destruction.

A master of contrasts, Raimund treats his audience to a comparison between the ruthless field marshal Phalarius and the amiable tailor Simplizius Zitternadel. Phalarius is drunk with power and fame; Simplizius, on the other hand, is given to the simple values in life. Phalarius gives the impression of being a hero, but is a coward at heart. Simplizius has great innate courage but appears a coward. Phalarius will do everything for fame and power; Simplizius does not know what to do when he is mistaken for a hero. Furthermore, a kinship exists between Simplizius and the barometer-maker Quecksilber in Raimund's first play. Both have grown out of the tradition of the Old Viennese Popular Theater; however, with Raimund's help, they have become more sophisticated and mundane than any of their predecessors.

Lucina's counterpart is Hades. Lucina represents the female of the species in a continuous matching of wits with Hades, the symbol of manhood. The eternal female battles the eternal male until Lucina's wiles win over Hades' power. Lucina is victorious because she has Virtue on her side. At the end of the play, the chorus intones:

"Hail Lucina! Hail Kreon!
Virtue joyously found its reward!" (II, 19)

The structure of the play is suggested by its title: *Die unheilbrigende Krone* refers to the tragic central action of this play, while the subtitle *König ohne Reich, Held ohne Mut, Schönheit ohne Jugend* relates to the three subplots. The overall plot is a mixture of tragic and comical elements that freely intermingle within the realms of reality and magic. Raimund wished to synthesize Greek and Roman antiquity with the Germanic fairytale world. In spite of the initially poor reception on the Viennese stage, *Die unheilbringende Krone* has been called a significant example of world drama by such reputed critics as Heinz Kindermann, Eduard Castle, and Karl Goedecke. It appeared at the Burgtheater on March 23, 1944, under the direction of Herbert Waniek, featuring Hermann Thimig in the role of Simplizius Zitternadel.[15] For the most recent productions, Oskar Kokoschka has designed some highly original scenery. In the same year in which Raimund's play appeared on the stage the Theater an der Wien produced a parody by Josef Schickh entitled *Die goldpapierne Zauberkrone oder nichts ist unmöglich* (*The Goldpaper Magic Crown or Nothing is Impossible*). In Raimund's time, this parody was considered by some to be on the same level as the original. Today it is totally unknown.

Looking back at the four plays by Raimund discussed in this chapter, we realize that he wanted to prove to his foes that he could create plays that could be performed in the traditional Old Viennese Popular Theater as well as at the respected Burgtheater. And this he did accomplish. With none of these works does he abandon the Old Viennese Popular Theater; he rather attempts to raise the literary level to that of the classics of world drama. While willing to learn not only from Shakespeare, but also from Grillparzer, Calderón, and others, Raimund invented in these four plays his own plots and characters which felicitously combine reality and magic. Then he proceeded to inject these plays with the notion that the poetic imagination can serve as a model of justice, truth, and beauty for everyday reality.

CHAPTER 5

Imaginative Old Viennese Popular Theater

RUDOLF STEINKELLER, the new owner of the Leopold-städter Theater, appointed Raimund artistic director of his theater in April of 1828. Deeply honored by this, Raimund, in turn, promised to set the highest standards of performance. Unfortunately, these aspirations were not shared by Steinkeller, who was primarily interested in making money and cared little about personal relationships between the actors and the public. The general atmosphere at the Leopoldstädter Theater was getting progressively worse. The morale of the ensemble was at a low point. Such circumstances prompted Raimund to take a leave of absence for the purpose of rest and, possibly, to write another play.

I *The Mountain King and the Misanthrope*

While at Brühl and Johannstein, sometime between the beginning of May and the end of June, 1828, Raimund composed *Der Alpenkönig und der Menschenfeind.* Soon after his return to Vienna, he began to make arrangements for the elaborate stage scenery needed for this play. It opened on October 17, 1828, at the Leopoldstädter Theater and was a great hit with the audiences. Raimund himself played the role of the misanthrope Herr von Rappelkopf. On June 1, 1829, a magic pantomime by Ferdinand Occioni with the same title as Raimund's play appeared at the Josefstädter Theater. While the pantomime was soon forgotten, Raimund's play had its one hundredth performance on February 25, 1833.

A literary debate soon ensued concerning the relation of Raimund's work to Shakespeare's *Timon of Athens*, Molière's *Le Misanthrope*, and Schiller's fragment "Der Menschenfeind." [1] Grillparzer thought that not even Molière could have conceived a more effective plot than that which concerned the life of an Austrian madcap misanthrope.[2] More significant than the above argument is the fact that *Der Alpenkönig und der Menschenfeind* exists, and that it constitutes Raimund's singular contribution to world drama.

Wenzel Müller's overture establishes the mood for the opening of the play, set in an Alpine region that is ruled by the mountain king Astragalus. With his fourth and current wife, Antonie-Sophie,[3] the misanthrope Herr von Rappelkopf has gone into seclusion to escape from other human beings, whom he hates and fears. Rappelkopf's only daughter must keep her love for August Dorn a secret, for her father would never understand it. Rappelkopf is supicious of everyone around him, including his wife and his servants Lieschen and Habakuk. Once, when he sees Habakuk with a knife in his hand, he imagines that his wife might have dispatched the latter to assassinate him. After breaking all the furniture in the house, he stalks out and runs into the woods. There Rappelkopf encounters the charcoal burner Christian Glühwurm, his wife Martha, and the children Salchen, Hansel, Christopherl, and Andresel, as well as a grandmother, all of whom live in a secluded, dilapidated hut. This isolated retreat appeals to Rappelkopf, and he persuades these impoverished people to sell it to him for a good price. One day he meets the mountain king Astragalus, who tells him that he himself is to blame for his misanthropy, and sets out to prove it. In the process of self-examination, Rappelkopf can see himself in a double image and recognizes that he himself has been to blame for all his difficulties. He becomes a reformed misanthrope, and gives his blessing to the marriage of his daughter Malchen and her young suitor August Dorn. Peace and tranquillity seem to have settled upon the house of Rappelkopf, as he makes a final statement about the importance of knowing and understanding one's self:

> Oh, recognition, incomparable star,
> Not ev'ry one seeks thee, for some wish thee far,
> There are, for example, the ones who betray.
> If insight they wanted, the truth they would say.
>
> But first let us mention girls fair as the moon,
> The ones we men always recognize soon.

We're slower the praises of good girls to sing.
But once they are known, only joy do they bring.

A young man so often desires recognition,
And swallows things whole to attain this condition.
But let him just wait till old age arrives,
And for recognition he won't have to strive.

A man should at first just himself seek to know,
A precept the oldest philosophers show.
And all men can say, if their faults they will trace,
I've seen my own nature, I know my true face.

Above all our art recognition desires,
This dainty coquette to your favor aspires.
And if she today little glory did show,
At least we can hope that her will you did know! (II, 15)

The popular reception of this play can be attributed to Raimund's portrayal of himself in the character of Rappelkopf. Both have uncontrollable tempers and find it difficult to get along with other people. Nevertheless, this therapeutic exercise in self-analysis did not cause Raimund to give up his misanthropy any more than it did Rappelkopf. With both, misanthropy was deeply ingrained and could be only temporarily suppressed; but there was always the danger that it might erupt again. At the end of his self-analysis, Rappelkopf becomes a "reformed misanthrope," as did Raimund for a while, until he could no longer suppress it and committed suicide. Upon Grillparzer's advice, Raimund attempted to write another piece with a similar theme, to be called "Eine Nacht am Himalaja" ("A Night in the Himalayas"). However, this project never emerged beyond its initial stages.

Lord Philip Henry Stanhope (1787–1855) came to Vienna and saw Raimund perform in his *Der Alpenkönig und der Menschenfeind*, liked it, and decided to translate the play into English.[4] He gave this translation to Frederick Yates, manager of the Adelphi Theater in London, who in turn requested the actor John Baldwin Buckstone to adapt it for the stage. In his adaptation, Buckstone omitted several scenes with the mountain king because he thought they would not appeal to English audiences. For these scenes he substituted a melodramatic subplot. Buckstone's adaptation was given as *The King of the Alps and the Misanthrope* on January 24, 1831, at the Adelphi Theater, with Charles Matthews as Rappel-kopf, and Henry Yates as the mountain king. This adaptation was to popular that it ran for over three months without interruption. The "Tattler" and "Literary Gazette" praised the production, and the "Court Journal" compared it to Goethe's *Faust.* A textual comparison between Raimund's original and Buckstone's adaptation was made by Robert F. Arnold, who carefully documented the changes wrought in the original.[5]

In this play, Raimund touched upon the universal dilemma that concerns the struggle between the universal order and the individual ego. Corruption and injustice have been part of this universal order ever since its inception. Convinced of this, Raimund wanted to create a poetic image that did contain order and justice.

On a personal level, Rappelkopf's behavior represents Raimund's own inner conflicts. The first step toward amelioration is to determine which game of life is being played.[6] Self-recognition may lead to eventual recovery, or to an intensification of the malady. With Rappelkopf, the process becomes suspended at the point of self-recognition; with Raimund, self-recognition is only temporary. Heinz Politzer sees this play as a tragic comedy of skepticism.[7] Convinced that evil is an integral part of the world, Rappelkopf does not seek a solution in his environment, but in his own soul. One of the evils is the corruptibility of money, particularly since with it Rappelkopf does the charcoal burner's family out of their lifelong possession.

On an abstract level, the play becomes a confrontation of the uninhibited and irresponsible ego with the will of the world. In a test of strength between these two, the will of the world will usually win out in the end. The ego then has the choice of either recognizing the situation and adapting to it or being crushed by the powerful forces of the will of the world. Since Raimund was not beyond being didactic, Rappelkopf's comprehension of himself and his relationship to the world may be looked upon as an expression of skepticism in the ways of the world, that can only be counteracted by one's own adaptability.

Basically a good Christian, Raimund saw nature as a beautiful and ordered creation of God. In contrast to the perfection found in nature, civilization was man-made and highly imperfect. It is for this reason that Raimund sends Rappelkopf into the forest where nature, as he understood it, was not disturbed by civilization. Once this is accomplished with the aid of the allegorical mountain king, Rappelkopf may return to his family and assume his place in society.

Rappelkopf's wife Antonie-Sophie is a pillar of society and shows a close resemblance to Raimund's common-law wife, Toni. Both stood for what was proper and reasonable in life, and both lacked a certain sense of humor, always taking things very seriously. They suffered their fate with humility and considered it a just reward for their way of life.

The traditional Old Viennese Popular Theater receives its due with the appearance of the servants Lieschen and Habakuk in Rappelkopf's house. Their personalities are more fully developed than those of their comical predecessors, and they play a more important and integral part in the action of the play. Lieschen is sufficiently emancipated to engage Rappelkopf in a conversation, as he appears in the disguise of his brother-in-law:

LISA

The mistress asks if you'd like to have a cup of tea, sir.

RAPPELKOPF

No, thank you. (*To himself*) I'll put her through the mill too. (*Aloud*) What's my sister doing?

LISA

She's very worried.

RAPPELKOPF

About what?

LISA

About the master.

RAPPELKOPF

About me?

LISA

Oh no, not about you.

RAPPELKOPF
(Catching himself)
Oh, of course. *(To himself)* She doesn't recognize me either. *(Aloud)*
And what is my niece doing?

LISA
She's talking with her fiancé.

RAPPELKOPF
(To himself) Heaven and Hell! *(Composing himself)* What sort of
man is he?

LISA
A very nice man.

RAPPELKOPF
What do you mean? Is he courting you too?

LISA
That I'd like to see—he hardly dares even look at another girl. He'll
be a real gem to have around the house. I think he hasn't given me
a single tip, just in order to keep from touching my hand. He and
the young mistress were just made for each other, and it's a crying
shame that the master won't give his consent.

RAPPELKOPF
(Quickly)
And he's perfectly right. The young man doesn't respect him.

LISA
Oh my, he values him much more highly—if you'll excuse me for
talking about your brother-in-law this way, sir—much more highly
than he deserves.

RAPPELKOPF
(To himself)
It seems they've all been plotting against me. Patience, don't desert
me! *(Aloud)* I'm going to give you a tip, but first tell me quickly all
the bad qualities of your master.

LISA
Quickly, sir? That's impossible.

RAPPELKOPF

Why?

LISA

Because if I start right this minute, I still wouldn't be finished by tomorrow morning.

RAPPELKOPF

I wish I knew where I find the patience to listen to all this!

LISA

It's enough that he's a misanthrope. I just don't understand how anyone with such a large fortune, such a good-natured wife, such a well-brought-up daughter, and such a pretty chambermaid, could be a misanthrope.

(Song)
Oh, the world is gay and cheerful,
And our life can be so fair.
There's no reason to be fearful,
Meeting joy with hateful stare.
Ev'rything shows pleasing features,
All the world unites in hope,
But the ugliest of creatures,
Surely is the misanthrope.

Happy spirits bring us pleasure,
Joy makes music fill the air,
Love to all is richest treasure,
Hatred only brings despair.
But while others evil scorn,
Laughing hearts so full of hope,
In the woods, by hatred torn,
Sits alone our misanthrope.

See the sun with rays so golden,
Proudly in the heavens rise.
All mankind he does embolden,
Fills with purest joy the skies.
Why should we the world be hating,
When its beauty all can see?
If your love is unabating,
Misanthrope you'll never be. (II, 7)

Habakuk is no pushover either. Whenever he does not receive the full measure of respect he feels he deserves, he does not hesitate to remind one that: "I've already spent two years in Paris!"

The mountain king Astragalus represents a stark contrast to Rappelkopf. He is the embodiment of friendliness and compassion. Astragalus explains his existence as a means of helping human beings to better understand themselves. For that purpose, he has established a "Temple of Self-Recognition." His intention is to lead Rappelkopf to that place. Once he has accomplished his mission, Astragalus vanishes back into the eternal folds of nature whence Raimund had fetched him to bring Rappelkopf to his senses.

The scene with Rappelkopf in the charcoal burner's hut, has been called a precursor of Naturalism in German drama.[8] Its humor is wrought out of a tragic alienation and elemental human needs, and is worthy of reproduction here:

RAPPELKOPF
Hey, there's a show! Hit him harder! What rabble! (*Coming to the middle of the room and clapping his hands. Maliciously*) Bravo! Bravissimo!

SALLY
Look at him. What's he want here?

MARTHA
What do you want? What're you looking at?

RAPPELKOPF
Not you, you old hag! What's the hut here cost? How much do I have to pay to throw you all out?

SALLY
Huh, he's got funny ideas.

MARTHA
You nosy old man, what do you mean, comin' in here—

SALLY
And insultin' us.

[96]

CHRISTIAN
(*Half asleep*)

Throw'm out!

MARTHA
(*Ill-temperedly*)

Shut up! (*To Rappelkopf*) Whatta you mean, givin' orders? I'll beat my kids whenever I want.

ANDRES

Yeah, whatta you care about my head? We get beatin's for dinner here.

THE BOY UNDER THE BED

Get him, boy!

THE DOG

Bow, wow!

MARTHA AND SALLY

Get outa here!

RAPPELKOPF

Quiet! Not another word! (*Pulls out two purses and shakes them*) Here's money! Here are gold pieces! They're all yours. Got it? So be friendly, smile, say sir. Hurry! Baggage! Quick!

MARTHA

Oh, sir, please forgive us. Go on, children, kiss the gentleman's hand. Maybe he'll give you something.
(*The children creep out*)

ANDRES
(*Laughing stupidly*)

He's got gold? Come on, boys, let's kiss his hand.
(*They kiss his hands*)

RAPPELKOPF

There comes the pack already.

THE THREE BOYS

Mister, give me a piece, please, please.

CHRISTIAN
Bring me some too!

SALLY
Aren't you ashamed? He's makin' fools of you!

RAPPELKOPF
What do you want for this hole, old lady? I'll buy it. No matter what it costs.

MARTHA
Oh, sir, you must be kiddin'. What'd you want with this rotten hut?

RAPPELKOPF
None of your business. Is two hundred gold pieces enough?

MARTHA
Oh, my, sir! There ain't that much dough in the world, we'd be fixed for the rest of our days!

SALLY
Mama, you wouldn't sell the hut? What'll Franz say when he hears it?

ANDRES
Mama, give it to him, it's not worth that much.

MARTHA
Oh, my God, what a break! If I could only talk it over with my man.

ANDRES
Daddy! Get up! Or we'll sell the house and you with it.

MARTHA
You, husband! (*To herself*) Oh, the shame of it, in front of strangers! He can't even move. (*During this speech, the dog rubs against Rappelkopf, who kicks it away. The dog barks at him. Martha says aloud*) You can sell the hut, imagine, we'll get two hundred gold pieces for it.

CHRISTIAN
It ain't enough—ain't enough.

SALLY
If only he won't do it!

MARTHA

My man don't know what he's sayin'. You can have it sir, it's okay.

RAPPELKOPF

I'll take everything, just as it stands.

MARTHA

There's a little kitchen outside, with lots of dishes.

ANDRES

And mice, they're free.

RAPPELKOPF

There's the money. (*Throws the money to them*) Now get right out of here. All of you. In two minutes I want you all gone.

SALLY

You see, mama, he's tossin' us out already.
(*During these lines the children have gradually cleared everything away so that the front of the stage is free of furniture, except for one chair, on which Rappelkopf sits.*)
Enter Franz.)

FRANZ

Evenin' all, here's Franz!

RAPPELKOPF

There comes another one of these subhumans.

SALLY

Oh, Franz dear, just look at this stranger who bought the hut from mama. He's tossin' us all out. He paid her already.

FRANZ

Why, mother, what're you thinkin' of? Just give him back his money —he looks awful mean!

MARTHA

Oh, no—I'll never give it back, we'll never find anybody this dumb again. Just hush up, with this money you can get married.

SALLY

But where'll we sleep? It's almost night already.

MARTHA

For money they'll let us in anywhere. Hey, kids, papa, mama, get up!
We got to go.

ANDRES

Movin' out, movin' out! What fun!

MARTHA

Get up, man! (*She pulls him up and leads him forward*)

RAPPELKOPF

Is he sick?

MARTHA

I'll say.

RAPPELKOPF

Very long?

MARTHA

Oh, yes, it's an old complaint, it started last year.

RAPPELKOPF

That's a lie! That started last night! Get him out of here!

CHRISTIAN

Won't go till I got the dough. I'm a man, I got some sense in my
head, and I want something in my pocket too.

MARTHA

I got the money (*Puts his coat and hat on him*) so get moving! Come
on, kids, get the stuff together. (*Hans ties the dog to a cord*) Christopher, you lead grandma. (*They lift the old woman out of the bed
and put her crutch in her hand. To Hans*) You lead the dog, and I'll
lead my man.

RAPPELKOPF

And the baby? What about it?

ANDRES

I'll take it under my arm.

RAPPELKOPF

They're a bunch of hottentots. All ready now?

ANDRES

All hitched up.

RAPPELKOPF

Then drive away!

SALLY

So we really have to leave our dear home . . .

CHRISTOPHER
(*Crying*)

Where we were all born and raised.

SALLY

Honest, sir, you can't imagine what a lot of harm you're doing with all your money.

SALLY

And so farewell our little home,
So full of care we have to roam.

ALL
(*Except Rappelkopf*)

And so farewell, our little home,
So full of care we have to roam.

SALLY

No matter how our fortunes grow,
We'll think of you where'er we go.

ALL

No matter how our fortunes grow,
We'll think of you where'er we go.

(*They exit, two by two*)
(*They look around sadly as they go, including the dog*)

It may be useful, at this point, to analyze the relationship between Raimund's *Der Alpenkönig und der Menschenfeind*, its possible sources, and other manifestations of the misanthrope theme in world literature. Otto Rommel suggests that Alois Gleich's *Der Berggeist oder Die drei Wünsche* (*The Mountain Spirit or The Three Wishes*), 1819, served as a general model for

Raimund's play and other plays whose purpose concerned the curing of malcontents or human beings in need of help.[9] In this play Herr von Missmut, a rich landowner, is dissatisfied with his life. The mountain ghost cures Missmut by convincing him that happiness does not result from wealth and luxury, but rather from modesty and honesty. Missmut begins to accept the folly of his excesses and is cured: "Yes children, I'm back again, and have become much smarter. I have been cured of my stupidities and now I am ready to live with you all in happy harmony." (III, 15) When Rappelkopf is cured, he says something very similar: "Children, I'm a reformed misanthrope; stay with me and I will live out my life in the Temple of Self-Recognition." (II, 15) Gleich's frame of action in *Der Berggeist* may have served as a model not only for Raimund's *Der Alpenkönig und der Menschenfeind*, but also for Nestroy's *Lumpazivagabundus*, Grillparzer's *Der Traum ein Leben*, and others.

As a young man, Raimund saw many plays at the Burgtheater; among these was Kotzebue's *Menschenhass und Reue* (*Human Hatred and Repentance*), a drama of adultery, in which husband and wife are eventually brought together again. It suggests a distant parallel with Raimund's play, though it may have induced him to give the matter more thought, before the theme crystallized sufficiently to become the basis of the play.

Schiller's dramatic fragment "Der [vorsöhnte] Menschenfeind" [10] (The [reconciled] Misanthrope) may or may not have come to the attention of Raimund. The theme of Schiller's fragment suggests that the Creator made the world and man corrupted it. It seems to have been influenced by the thinking of Jean Jacques Rousseau. Schiller's misanthrope is Herr von Huten, who is certain that the whole human race is against him: "The whole human race is my murderer." (I, 8) It is never quite clear how Herr von Huten became a misanthrope who devotes all his time to his daughter Angelika. Although an interesting version of the misanthrope theme, Schiller's fragment is not sufficiently worked out to have had more than a passing influence on Raimund's play.

Molière's *Le Misanthrope*, completed around 1666, shows certain features prominent in Raimund's *Der Alpenkönig und der Menschenfeind*. Both playwrights wrote their respective plays with their heart and soul rather than their imagination. Both suffered from the impertinence and arrogance of those around them. Both were basically unhappy in their love life. Molière had married Armande Béjard, a beautiful actress, who was much younger than he, and very fickle. Raimund's relationship with Toni Wagner was frequently the source of mental anguish for both.

Le Misanthrope deals with pathetic jealousy cured when the hero finds out that his jealousy is completely unfounded. The hero is the irascible and irritable Alceste, who is frightfully jealous of Célimène. When Alceste speaks of himself, it might as well have been Molière: "Heaven has not given me a soul which is at home in a royal court. I do not have the virtues needed to make my sojourn here a success. My greatest talent is to be frank and upright. I can't deceive people while talking to them, and he that cannot hide what he thinks will make a very short stay in such quarters." (III, 7) Alceste is not on friendly terms with those he assails, while Célimène makes cruel sport of people she receives at her home with tokens of love and respect. Whatever Alceste says or does only serves to increase Célimène's diffidence; and this, in turn, makes him more savage. Although the mood of Molière's and Raimund's plays is the same, each is executed differently. Alceste must learn to fight the decadence and corruption of his society, which will allow him to exist only as a hypocrite. Rappelkopf, on the other hand, lives in a society that is receptive to him. Rappelkopf's problems do not emanate from his environment, but from within himself. His problems persist as long as he does not wish to control his vile temperament. At the end of the play, Rappelkopf is sufficiently cured to return to society. Alceste cannot change his corrupt environment and gradually succumbs to it. The writing of his play had a therapeutic effect on Raimund; for Molière it must have been sheer torture, because his unfaithful actress-wife played on stage the same infamous role she had been playing all along in real life.

Shakespeare's *Timon of Athens* was familiar to Raimund from his visits to the Burgtheater. Shakespeare reportedly derived his material from Plutarch's *Life of Anthony* and Lucian's dialogue, *Timon the Misanthrope*. The play depicts three kinds of misanthropy: Apemantus, the professional misanthrope, who refuses to admit the possibility of human virtue; Alcibiades, the unrelenting pessimist, who has a high opinion of himself; and Timon, the idealist, whose experience turns him into a misanthrope. Like King Lear, Timon experiences a shock of disillusionment; however, unlike Lear, his conduct is the logical result of his lack of wisdom. To Timon, universal nature is a place where "each thing's a thief." He acts according to his conviction that there is nothing but villainy in the world. He is much more demonic and incorrigible than Rappelkopf, and his misanthropy persists unto his grave. The literary device of confronting Rappelkopf with his own double image, in order to make him recognize the folly of misanthropy still remains within the realm of comprehensible human experience, whereas Timon's destructive attitude toward all living things becomes an abstract manifestation of misanthropy turned into pure evil.

Raimund's positive approach to the problems confronting the misanthrope Rappelkopf is more enlightening and humanistically more rewarding than that of Shakespeare. Over the past centuries, Shakespeare's *Timon of Athens* and Molière's *Le Misanthrope* have had a wider distribution than Raimund's *Der Alpenkönig und der Menschenfeind;* however, this in no way detracts from the Austrian dramatist's singular literary accomplishment. A significant feature of Raimund's work is that it is more appropriate to the mood and spirit of the twentieth century than are its more famous predecessors.

II *The Spendthrift*

Sometime around October, 1833, Raimund commenced to write his next and last play, which was initially entitled *Bilder aus dem Leben eines Verschwenders* (*Pictures from the Life of a Spendthrift*). When the work was completed, by December, Raimund renamed it *Der Verschwender*. It opened at the Josefstädter Theater on February 20, 1834, with Raimund in the role of the servant Valentin. The room in Gaaden in which Raimund wrote the "Hobellied" has been made into a museum by the *Raimundgesellschaft*.[11] This play is Raimund's most widely performed work, the first one, as a matter of fact, to be performed at the Burgtheater.

Much has been written about the possible sources Raimund

used in composing *Der Verschwender.* Eduard Castle pointed to
Shakespeare's *Timon of Athens,* Carlo Goldoni's *Il prodigo,* and
Philippe Néricault Destouches' *Le dissipateur ou l'honnête friponne.* Richard Smekal believed he had found the source in the
short story "Der junge Verschwender und seine Frau," which appeared in the *Taschenbuch des Theaters in der Leopoldstadt auf
das Jahr 1829,* and was, in part, based on Destouches' play. Gustav Pichler[12] agreed with Smekal's findings, but also considered
Hermine Cloeter's *Häuser und Menschen von Wien* (*Houses and
People of Vienna*), published in 1917, and suggested Johann
Heinrich von Geymüller as Raimund's life-size model for his character Flottwell. Although there is a reference to Geymüller in
Bäuerle's novel *Ferdinand Raimund* (I, 212–215), there is little
reason to believe that he actually served as a model for Flottwell.
Otto Rommel disputed Smekal's conclusions, without offering any
alternatives.[13] Heinz Kindermann only lightly touches upon the
question of origins and suggests that Raimund's play was the cul-
mination of precursors that started with the "Story of the Rich
Man" in the Middle Ages, and continued on by way of Shakespeare, Goldoni, and Destouches to Raimund.[14] Rudolf Fürst
looked for the origins in the Old Viennese Popular Theater tradition, specifically in Bäuerle's *Die natürliche Zauberei* (*Natural
Magic*) and Meisl's *Ein Tag in Wien* (*A Day in Vienna*)—plays
that are concerned with the sudden acquisition of wealth—as well
as plays like Bäuerle's *Der Freund in der Not* (*Friend in Distress*)
and Gleich's *Die Bedienten in Wien* (*Servants in Vienna*).[15] Erdmann indicated Leopold Huber's *Das Sternenmädchen im Meid-
linger Walde* (*The Star Girl in the Meidling Forest*) as the source
of the Cheristane Motif.[16] The name Cheristane itself was probably derived from Carlo Gozzi's fairytale "Woman as Serpent," in
which the character Cherestrani plays a significant role. Erdmann
saw also a possible relationship between Raimund's play and August Wilhelm Iffland's comedy *Die Hagestolzen* (*The Bachelors*).

   After careful sifting, it might be concluded that Raimund was
certainly familiar with the various plays of the Old Viennese Popular Theater tradition. Goldoni's *Il prodigo,* and Destouches' *Le
dissipateur ou l'honnête friponne* may also have been familiar to
him. The short story "Der junge Verschwender and seine Frau,"
published in 1829 in the almanac of the Leopoldstädter Theater,

where he was active as actor-director, almost certainly came to his attention. *Timon of Athens* and other plays by Shakespeare gave Raimund an awareness of the possible scope of the spendthrift theme. All of these dramatic works invariably left an imprint on Raimund's poetic imagination; however his own version of *Der Verschwender*, if viewed as a literary entity, is an original creation.

The play is divided into three acts. The first act serves to introduce the theme and characters. The wealthy nobleman Julius von Flottwell is introduced to the audience by means of the reactions of his servants Fritz and Johann, and his secretary Wolf. Flottwell is careless with his money, inclined to do everything in a grand and luxurious manner, and leaves most decisions to his ignominious secretary Wolf. His circle of friends includes shallow admirers and thieves, among them the Chevalier Dumont, Herr von Pralling, Herr von Helm, and Herr von Walter. Forever subservient to Flottwell, and forever tyrannical with subordinates, Wolf is the incarnation of evil itself. Wolf's personality is spotlighted when he confers with the two architects Gründling and Sockel, who are bidding for a contract to build Flottwell's new castle. Wolf interviews Gründling to establish how much money he can extort from him and, when the latter does not offer the expected gratuity, Wolf turns to his competitor Sockel, who is better acquainted with the customs of bribery, and who promises to pay the largest amount.

When the servant Valentin appears on stage, it is like a ray of sunshine amidst grandeur and decadence. He appropriately enters with a song:

> Happy, lucky, without sorrow
> Do I live from day to day,
> There's no need for me to borrow,
> So a servant's life is gay.
> First, my figure is amazing,
> I've of beauty quite a shot,
> And the girls get weak from gazing
> At the money I have got.
>
> Second, I've no bad intention,
> I'm as gentle as a lamb;

If my brains I do not mention,
'Tis because I modest am.
Third, I have a special hobby,
Singing up to stars and moon.
You'll go rushing to the lobby,
When you hear my favorite tune.

Fourth, I've got some education,
I can read—and write—and count.
I'm a joiner by profession
And I'm polished all around.
Fifth-sixth-seventh-eighth-Oh, pity!
This must be the final rhyme,
And whoever heard my ditty
Will be glad and say, "It's time!" (I, 6)

Then Valentin chats with the chambermaid Rosa about life in Flottwell's fabulous castle. Flottwell not only associates with mortal human beings but also has Cheristane as a protective spirit. And when she has to be absent, there is always Azur, who appears as a beggar and collects gifts from Flottwell. There is one sport, namely hunting, that is very popular with the leisure class. In the "Hunting Song," Valentin reflects about that dubious sport:

Why do people rich and smart
Want to make their lives so hard?
'Stead of in their castle staying,
Dancing, or pinochle playing,
Out in any kind of weather
They go hunting for a feather,
Through the muddy gorges crawling
And a heavy rifle hauling.
Only fools exactly know
Why they all a-hunting go!

Three A.M. the bugle sounds,
Up get hunters and the hounds.
They start cleaning rifles busy,
I am still a little dizzy.
Then it's wholly to their liking
All day long through forests hiking,
Without eating, without resting,

Happy animals molesting.
You in heaven, you, O Lord,
Keep me out of such a sport.

No, for hunting I don't care!
They have chased me like a hare.
Over ev'ry root I've stumbled
And a thousand times I've stumbled.
All around the bullets flying,
In my mind I kept on dying.
Hunters ne'er will be forgiving.
Hunting is no job for me,
Ev'rybody must agree.

Tired and hungry as you feel,
You sit down to have a meal.
Nothing will disturb you now.
But there comes a monstrous sow!
You get up, and as you're standing
From all sides and without ending
Lions, tigers, come on jumping,
Into other beasts you're bumping,
And there isn't any fence—
No, for hunting I've no sense! (I, 14)

The fairy Cheristane reappears in a subsequent scene and discloses that she had provided Flottwell's father with the wealth which his son has now inherited. She was moved to do so by the sight of young Flottwell, whom she loved from that moment on. It was love in the form of "Caritas." Cheristane is disturbed that all that wealth had really become an obstacle in Flottwell's life and slowed his development towards full maturity. She can foretell how Flottwell is going to ruin himself, and dispatches her assistant, Azur, in the disguise of a beggar, giving Flottwell a foretaste of things to come unless he is willing to change his reckless ways. However, Flottwell does not understand the symbolic presence of the beggar, simply gives him some money and dismisses him.

In the second act, which takes place three years later, Flottwell is in pursuit of the desirable Amalia, daughter of the President von Klugheim. No expense is too great to win Amalia's favor. In a subplot, the Chevalier Dumont stumbles upon an old, toothless peasant woman, and believes he has encountered a piece of nature in the raw. The aged woman, in turn, is bewildered and amused by this unexpected attention. Corruption in the Flottwell household reaches a new high when the secretary Wolf dismisses Valentin and Rosa on trumped-up charges of theft. The true reason for the dismissal is that Rosa had thwarted Wolf's advances. There is a major crisis in Flottwell's life when Klugheim refuses to allow his daughter to marry the spendthrift; whereupon Flottwell packs up and escapes with Amalia to England. In London he loses much of his fortune. On a sea voyage to South America his wife and child are drowned, and Flottwell barely escapes with his own life.

In the third act, twenty years later, Flottwell appears as a beggar. From his former gardner he hears that his former secretary, Wolf, is the new owner of his castle. The only loyal human being turns out to be his former servant Valentin. In the meantime, Valentin has married Rosa and they have several children. After convincing his wife that this is the thing to do, Valentin asks the beggar Flotwell to stay at his home. Valentin has grown in maturity and expresses his new philosophy of life in the "Hobellied" ("Song of the Plane"), which has become popular in Austria:

> There are those people fightin' still
> For things that come and go;
> They call each other names at will,
> At th' end they nothing know.
> Here proudly rides too rich a man,
> The poorest there must hike,
> But Fate moves in and with its plane
> Planes rich and poor alike.
>
> The youth so happy and so bold
> Is always after fun,
> But let them get a little old,
> With less they'll carry on.
> My wife is sometimes raising hell!
> That doesn't bother me;
> I do my work, and do it well,
> And let her angry be.

If death appears—please do forgive—
And whispers, "Brother, come!"
I wish I could still longer live,
And act like deaf and dumb.
But says he, "My dear Valentine,
Come now with me to dwell,"
I put my plane into the shrine
And bid the world farewell! (III, 6)

Together with Valentin and his family, Flottwell spends the rest of his days in a modest manner on the income from all the gifts he had once carelessly heaped on Azur. There is enough money for Valentin's family and Flottwell to live out their lives without hardship.

The Hamburg theater impresario, Friedrich Ludwig Schmidt, opined that Flottwell deserved a happier ending than the one Raimund had provided for him. But Raimund confirmed that this was the only ending he intended. Flottwell could not possibly be restored to his original grandeur and decadence. All Raimund wished to show was that in his old age he would not be dependent on the mercy of his greedy fellowmen. Profligacy was to be condemned, and Flottwell deserved a chance to end his life like an ordinary citizen.

Flottwell is so wrapped up in himself that he does not recognize Valentin's loyalty until toward the end of his life. He has always taken Valentin for granted. When he finally notices Valentin's unselfishness, he is moved to exclaim: "Oh servant's fidelity! You are like the moon; we recognize you only when the sun has gone down." (III, 6) This ingratitude, which Valentin experienced all through his life, was not different from that which Raimund felt had been his lot. Valentin's precursors included Kratzerl, Kasperl, Thaddädl, and Hanswurst. However, none of these characters underwent as much change as Valentin. Raimund traced his development from carefree youth to responsible maturity.

The author's social consciousness brings about a synthesis between members of the lowest and highest social strata on a purely human level. The servant Valentin becomes a friend and possible provider of his former master, the nobleman Julius von Flottwell. The common denominator that brings them together is human dignity and compassion. The human level was the only valid basis of human relationships as far as Raimund was concerned. Although he knew it to be rarely possible in real life, he at least contrived such a situation in his ideal imagination for the stage.

Florian Waschblau, the servant in Raimund's second play, *Der Diamant des Geisterkönigs*, is a forerunner of Valentin. Both prove their loyalty and devotion to their masters by their willingness to go through water or fire for them, and sometimes literally so. Both servants have their special Viennese girl friends. Florian has his Mariandel and Valentin his Rosa. Valentin and Rosa make their relationship socially acceptable when they get married and raise a family. Raimund wished to demonstrate that Valentin, a mere servant, was a human being with a full range of human feelings and desires. This range of human characteristics had hitherto been reserved for people of wealth or noble birth. Raimund intimated that Valentin's low birth was no more an obstacle to human decency than Raimund's low birth had been to him.

The incarnation of evil and villainy in this play is Flottwell's secretary Wolf. Compared to Gluthahn in Raimund's earlier play *Moisasurs Zauberfluch*, who was brutally evil in an abstract way, Wolf is irredeemably so in every respect. Wolf's entire energy is cynically directed toward acquisition of wealth, power, and prestige, regardless of the cost. Forever attributing his evil motives to those around him, Wolf enriches himself to the point where he even takes possession of Flottwell's castle. Such a life gives him a troubled conscience and tormented soul and body in his old age. Raimund gives vent here to the pessimistic notion that certain evils can never be completely eradicated.

Fairies and ghosts play a minor part in Raimund's last play. The fairy Cheristane and her assistant, the protective spirit Azur, are unobtrusive. They have no power to change the course of fate, and can only use their good services to persuade. Cheristane's and Azur's absence would in no way alter the course of the action.

Der Verschwender has been most popular in the German-speaking countries. But it was not long before the play was translated into other European languages. Jan Stepánek made the first Czech translation in 1840, which he called *Marnotratnik*, and which formed the basis of an 1874 adaptation by Franz Novotny.[17] According to Heinz Kindermann,[18] an English translation was made in 1840 by a certain Mr. Smith, and was presumably produced in Philadelphia and on other stages where English was spoken.[19] O. Paul Straubinger reports that between 1842 and 1911 the German stage in St. Louis performed *Der Verschwender* no less than thirty-four times.[20] The German Theater at San Francisco also recorded performances of this piece between 1861 and 1864. There seems to have existed a copyrighted English translation of the work by Thomas E. Van Bibber in 1884, but somehow, all traces of it seem lost.

Raimund's *Der Verschwender*, more than any of his previous plays, made him internationally known in his own lifetime. But being famous could not cure him of occasional melancholy and depression. Nestroy's rise in the literary horizon began secretly to irritate him. When Nestroy's *Lumpazivagabundus* was given in 1833, Raimund went to see it, and abhorred it. The title alone turned his stomach upside-down. Raimund could feel in every bone of his body that his style and era were coming to an end, and that Nestroy's sarcastic wit was winning new friends by the day. For some time Raimund had been hearing about Nestroy's appearance in his own favorite roles of King Tutu, Fortunatus Wurzel, Rappelkopf, Nachtigall, Florian, and Gluthahn.[21] Raimund didn't like what he heard. He was deeply hurt that Nestroy interpreted his favorite roles in a more vulgar and cynical manner than he had intended. Nestroy was not only making a name for himself as an actor, but also as a playwright. In less than twenty months, Nestroy flooded the stages with eleven of his plays. His output as a writer by far surpassed Raimund's in quantity; however, the same could not be said about the literary quality. The Stagecoach Age was being replaced by the Steam Engine Age. Raimund's charming era of the real and imaginary worlds was drawing to an end as a more aggressive age was rushing in on him from all sides. Leisure and finesse were being replaced by frenzy and coarseness. It was time to make room for a new generation.

CHAPTER 6

Raimund's Place in Literature

RAIMUND'S Austria was personified by Klemens Metternich, who became his country's foreign minister in 1809, and for four decades represented Austria in European affairs. Metternich's diplomatic skill made Austria into a model of European order after Napoleon's downfall. The Congress of Vienna, 1814–1815, which attempted to restore the *status quo* in Europe, was the symbol of his achievements. Metternich's conservatism was based on the theory that peace and order could be secured only by an immutable maintenance of existing conditions. Espionage, censorship, and repression of liberal movements were essential features of his policy. Life in Austria was dominated by the aristocracy and a top-havy bureaucracy. Much of the energy of this bureaucracy went into manufacturing mountains of paper and fighting dangerous liberal thoughts. Although the importation of "questionable" foreign books was forbidden, the educated classes seemed aware of what was astir abroad. Such conditions led the populace to seek distraction in the theater. There it was possible to catch concealed allusions to the existing conditions of the land interspersed with fantastic fairy tales or harmless farces. The moral of most plays was that, however exciting other places around the world might be, Vienna was still the most delightful abode.

The chief literary reaction to the Metternich era was the Biedermeier spirit, characterized by passivity and resignation. This spirit dominated Austria's intellectual climate between 1820 and 1840. It emphasized bourgeois virtues, simple domestic joys, and a quiet acceptance of authority. The dualism of life, which Classicism and Romanticism attempted to conquer, underwent a synthesis and conciliation in the Biedermeier. The antipode to the

Biedermeier mood was the activism of the "Young Germany" movement.

Raimund entered the theater as an actor in his early youth, and became a playwright almost unintentionally. In his attempt to synthesize dramatic values of the Old Viennese Popular Theater with those of the classical drama, Raimund succeeded in raising the former to new poetic heights, without abandoning his enhancement of the semiconscious longing of simple folk for recognition, human dignity, and justice.

Raimund obtained his effects by means of a picturesque, sometimes melancholy idiom, which combines the delightfully musical Viennese dialect with standard High German. Allegorical figures and characters from the Viennese milieu speak and act in a manner that suggests no division between the worlds of reality and imagination. The action in Raimund's plays is frequently treated from the vantage point of a naïve, almost child-like human being.

With Raimund the concept of morality is based on the wishful thinking that virtue should always be victorious over evil. Since society in Austria was inflexibly structured according to rank or station, rather than function, so that higher qualities were attributed instinctively to those whose position in society was more elevated, Raimund wished to restore to the average man an incentive for self-culture and give him an opportunity to assert his manhood and self-respect. He wished to emphasize that when it comes to relationships between human beings, character and human compassion are more important than station. Since his stage characters are varieties of the *genus homo,* rather than bearers of this or that title, his plays tend to be comedies of character rather than comedies of manners, making his images more a picture of universal humanity than of his contemporary society. Raimund's audiences were made to see the essential characteristics of humanity so clearly, that in their light the peculiar aspect of institutions tended to seem of relatively little importance. By his laughter, the average man consoled himself for his relative obscurity, and the nobleman for his relative nullity; and, at least for the duration of Raimund's plays, the balance of society was maintained.

Nursed in the tradition of the Old Viennese Popular Theater, which derived its sources from the Folk Play, the *Commedia dell'Arte,* the Jesuit Theater, the Baroque Court Opera, and the

English and German traveling theater companies, Raimund soon rose beyond its confines to the level of the classics. All his life he had been a student and admirer of Shakespeare, Schiller, Molière, Calderón, and Grillparzer. In tune with his time, Raimund incorporated into his work Romanticism's susceptibility to the world of fairy tales and the magic of nature, as well as the Biedermeier's predisposition for simplicity, modesty, and the comman man. Regretting the lack of a formal education, a fact that turned out both advantageous and disadvantageous to his development, Raimund was a self-made man, whose major concern was the need for human brotherhood transcending all social and political differences. His plays frequently mirror his own fears and desires, which he resolved more equitably in his plays than in real life. As a regenerator of his country's popular drama, he has become a national institution in Austria. Just as Austria is unthinkable without Raimund, so Raimund is unthinkable without Austria.

Notes and References

Chapter One

1. Leopold Schmidt, *Das deutsche Volksschauspiel* (Berlin, 1962). This book deals with the German folk play tradition, which flourished in Austria, Switzerland, and Germany. A very useful bibliography is found on pp. 353–459.
2. Ibid., p. 307.
3. Ibid., p. 328.
4. Ibid., p. 307.
5. The *Commedia dell'Arte*, in one form or another, also became popular in Germany, France, England, Spain, and Poland.
6. Josef Nadler, *Literaturgeschichte Österreichs* (Salzburg, 1951), p. 152.
7. Josef Gregor, *Das Österreichische Theater* (Vienna, 1948), p. 80.
8. Ibid., p. 81.
9. Josef Nadler, op. cit., p. 153.
10. Otto Rommel, *Die Alt-Wiener Volkskomödie* (Vienna, 1952), p. 109.
11. Josef Nadler, op. cit., p. 159.
12. For a list of sources of Stranitzky's works, see Otto Rommel, *Die Alt-Wiener Volkskomödie*, p. 232, footnote 112.
13. For a detailed discussion of a theory of comedy, see Otto Rommel, "Die wissenschaftlichen Bemühungen um die Analyse des Komischen," and "Komik und Lustspieltheorie," *Deutsche Vierteljahresschrift für Literaturwissenschaft und Geistesgeschichte*, XXI (1943), 161–195, and 252–286.
14. Otto Rommel, *Barocktradition im österreichisch-bayrischen Volkstheater* (Leipzig, 1935–1939), I, 33.
15. Ibid., I, 12–13.
16. Otto Rommel, *Die Alt-Wiener Volkskomödie*, p. 409.
17. Ibid., p. 395.
18. Anton Bauer, *Das Theater in der Josefstadt zu Wien* (Vienna, Munich, 1957), p. 26.
19. Otto Rommel, *Die Alt-Wiener Volkskomödie*, p. 642.
20. For a chronological list of Meisl's plays, see Otto Rommel, *Die Alt-Wiener Volkskomödie*, pp. 1043–1054.
21. Ibid., p. 680.

22. For a chronological list of Bäuerle's works, see ibid., pp. 1055–1061.

23. Gustav Gugitz, *Die Ehetragödie Ferdinand Raimunds* (Vienna, 1956), *passim*.

24. For a chronological list of Gleich's works, see Otto Rommel, *Die Alt-Wiener Volkskomödie*, pp. 1028–1043.

25. Otto Rommel, ed. *Johann Nestroy. Gesammelte Werke* (Vienna, 1962), I, 18.

26. Ibid., I, 63.

27. For a chronological list of Nestroy's works, see ibid., I, 190–193.

28. For a list of Comédie-Vaudeville originals that served as a basis for some of Nestroy's works, see ibid., I, 119–120.

Chapter Two

1. Before coming to Vienna, Ochsenheimer wrote the plays *Er soll sich schlagen* and *Die Einquartierung*, as well as the novel *Skizzen aus dem Menschenleben*. When not working in the theater, he was an amateur entomologist.

2. Wilhelm Börner, *Ferdinand Raimund* (Leipzig, 1905), p. 10.

3. Fritz Brukner and Eduard Castle, eds., *Ferdinand Raimund, Sämtliche Werke* (Vienna, 1924–1934), III, 289.

4. Gustav Pichler, ed., *Der unbekannte Raimund* (Vienna, 1962), p. 6.

5. There is some disagreement regarding the exact date: The definitive critical edition by Brukner and Castle, V, pt. 1, xi, suggests April 13 for Feldkümmel, and April 15 for Franz Moor; Otto Rommel, in *Die Alt-Wiener Volkskomödie*, p. 894, only mentions April; Anton Bauer, *Das Theater in der Josefstadt zu Wien* (Vienna, 1957), p. 37, gives May 13 and May 14; and Wilhelm Börner, *Ferdinand Raimund* (Leipzig, 1905), p. 18, lists April 13 for Feldkümmel.

6. Fritz Brukner and Eduard Castle, eds., *Sämtliche Werke* (Vienna, 1924–1934), V, pt. 1, 13.

7. Heinz Kindermann, *Ferdinand Raimund* (Vienna, Leipzig, 1940), p. 47.

8. Ibid., p. 92.

9. Costenoble's comedies were collected in the *Almanach dramatischer Spiele*, published in 1925. There is need for a further study of the influences of Costenoble's work upon that of Raimund.

10. Gustav Gugitz, *Die Ehetragödie Ferdinand Raimunds* (Vienna, 1956), pp. 25–30, contains biographical sketches of the many women who knew the prince.

11. There is some doubt that Amalia was really Raimund's daughter. See Gustav Gugitz, *Die Ehetragödie Ferdinand Raimunds,* p. 20. Wilhelm Börner, *Ferdinand Raimund,* p. 24, suggests that another child, Emilie, may have been born to Raimund and Luise.

12. Wilhelm Börner, *Ferdinand Raimund,* p. 37.

13 for Feldkümmel, and April 15 for Franz Moor; Otto Rommel, in

14. Erich Schmidt, *Charakteristiken* (Berlin, 1902), I, 397.

15. Robert F. Arnold, *Raimund in England* (Vienna, 1902), pp. 235–256.

Chapter Three

1. See the text of Raimund's plays in Fritz Brukner and Eduard Castle, eds. *Ferdinand Raimund Sämtliche Werke* (Vienna, 1924–1934), vols. I and II.

2. A further probing based on Eduard and Margarete Castle's researches concerning the texts of Raimund's works might provide further insight into the character of the changes made by the author throughout his life.

3. Christoph Martin Wieland, *Dschinnistan, oder auserlesene Feen- und Geistermärchen* (*Winterthur,* 1810), III, 66–98.

4. Heinz Kindermann, *Ferdinand Raimund,* p. 130.

5. Gustav Pichler, ed., *Der unbekannte Raimund,* p. 7.

6. The second source is suggested in Rudolf Fürst's introduction to his edition of Raimund's works (Berlin, Leipzig, Vienna, Stuttgart, 1909), I, xxxiii.

7. The third source was suggested in the "Textgestaltungen" of Raimund's works edited by Fritz Brukner and Eduard Castle (Vienna, 1924–1934).

8. Otto Rommel, *Barocktradition im österreichisch-bayrischen Volkstheater* (Leipzig, 1935–1939), III, 41.

9. *Ferdinand Raimund,* p. 176.

10. Gustav Pichler, ed., *Der unbekannte Raimund,* p. 7.

11. See the German translation of Andersen's adaptation in Gustav Pichler, ed., *Raimund Almanach* (Vienna, 1963), pp. 7–70.

Chapter Four

1. Text variations in *Der Bauer als Millionär* are contained in *Sämtliche Werke,* ed. Friedrich Schreyvogl (Munich, 1960), pp. 607–639.

2. See Rudolf Prisching, "Raimunds Mädchen aus der Feenwelt," *Alt-Wiener Kalender* (Vienna, 1926), pp. 90–114.

3. *Ferdinand Raimund Die gefesselte Phantasie,* ed. Gustav Pichler (Vienna, 1960), p. 81.

4. See Heinz Kindermann's introduction to *Die gefesselte Phantasie* (Graz, 1957), pp. 5–27.

5. Walter Erdmann, *Ferdinand Raimund* (Würzburg, 1943), p. 132.

6. *Ferdinand Raimunds Werke,* ed. Rudolf Fürst (Berlin, Leipzig, Vienna, Stuttgart, 1909), p. lxv.

7. Eugen Kilian, "Raimunds *Gefesselte Phantasie* im neuen musikalischen Gewande," *Jahrbuch der Grillparzer-Gesellschaft,* (1902), p. 196.

8. For further reading on this subject, see A. Leslie Willson, *A Mythical Image: The Ideal of India in German Romanticism* (Durham, N. C., 1964).

9. Heinz Kindermann, *Ferdinand Raimund,* p. 314, also p. 319.

10. Karl Gladt, "*Moisasurs Zauberfluch—Moisasuras Hexenspruch:* Eine vergleichende Betrachtung," *Raimund-Almanach,* ed. Gustav Pichler (Vienna, 1963), pp. 83–106.

11. After serving as theatrical director in Linz, Agram, and Trieste, Börnstein moved in 1849 to the United States, where from 1859 to 1861 he directed the German Theater in St. Louis and presumably also produced plays by Raimund. Between 1869 and 1871, he was active at the Josefstädter Theater.

12. *Moisasurs Zauberfluch,* ed. Gustav Pichler (Zurich, Leipzig, Vienna, 1958).

13. *Moisasurs Zauberfluch,* ed. Gustav Pichler (Vienna, 1960). See the costume and scenery sketches by Oskar Kokoschka, pp. 314–315.

14. The equally authentic alternate title is *Die unheilbringende Zauberkrone oder König ohne Reich, Held ohne Mut, Schönheit ohne Jugend.* The word "Zauber" was added by the censors.

15. See *Ferdinand Raimund Die unheilbringende Krone,* ed. Gustav Pichler (Vienna, 1959), theater bill of the premiere, pp. 112–113.

Chapter Five

1. A quick survey shows that Heinz Kindermann, *Ferdinand Raimund,* p. 356, considers Raimund's *Der Alpenkönig und der Menschenfeind* superior to Shakespeare's, Molière's, and Schiller's works Wilhelm Bolin in "Der Menschenfeind: Eine literarhistorische Studie," *Euphorion* (1912), pp. 323–334, consider's Raimund's work more significant than Shakespeare's *Timon of Athens* and Schiller's fragment, and equal to Molière's *Le Misanthrope.* Walter Erdmann, *Ferdinand*

Notes and References

Raimund, pp. 148–180, regards Shakespeare's and Molière's works superior to that of Raimund. Heinz Politzer, in "Ferdinand Raimunds *Menschenfeind*," *Die Neue Rundschau* (1955), pp. 1–15, suggests that nowhere did Raimund come closer than in this play to the literary level of Shakespeare and Molière. Each of the above writers documents his findings in detail.

2. See *Der Alpenkönig und der Menschenfeind*, ed. Gustav Pichler (Vienna, 1959), pp. 112–114.

3. The editors disagree on the name of Rappelkopf's wife; some call her Antonie (e.g. Pichler), others Sophie (e.g. Rommel, Brukner and Castle, etc.). Raimund had apparently used both names to designate the same character, alternating them from manuscript to manuscript.

4. See Robert F. Arnold, "Ferdinand Raimund in England," p. 235, footnote 1, gives Josef Damse's first Polish translation of Raimund's work as *Chlop milionowy czyli dziewczyna ze swiata czarownego*, 1829, 1830.

5. See O. Paul Straubinger, "The Reception of Raimund and Nestroy in England and America" in *Österreich und die angelsächsische Welt: Kulturbegegnungen und Vergleiche*, ed. Otto Hietsch (Vienna, Stuttgart, 1961), pp. 481–494.

6. Eric Berne, in his book *Games People Play* (New York, 1964), would probably call it the "Kick-me Game."

7. Heinz Politzer, "Ferdinand Raimunds *Menschenfeind*," *Die Neue Rundschau* (1955), p. 13.

8. Heinz Kindermann, *Ferdinand Raimund*, pp. 365–366.

9. Otto Rommel, *Die Alt-Wiener Volkskomödie*, p. 819 ff.

10. Gustav Pichler includes Schiller's fragment in his edition of *Der Alpenkönig und der Menschenfeind* (Vienna, 1959), pp. 118–144.

11. See *Der Verschwender*, ed. Gustav Pichler (Vienna, 1958), p. 9 ff.

12. "Raimunds Verschwender und seine Vorfahren," ibid., pp. 9–13.

13. Otto Rommel, *Die Alt-Wiener Volkskomödie*, p. 925, footnote 13.

14. Heinz Kindermann, *Ferdinand Raimund*, p. 430.

15. Ferdinand Raimund, *Sämlichte Werke*, ed. R. Fuerst (Berlin, Leipzig, Vienna, Stuttgart, 1909), pp. lxxxiii–lxxxiv.

16. Walter Erdmann, *Ferdinand Raimund*, pp. 224 ff.

17. See Robert F. Arnold, "Ferdinand Raimund in England," p. 235, footnote 1.

18. Heinz Kindermann, *Ferdinand Raimund*, p. 429.

19. Straubinger doubts the accuracy of this contention because of the lack of English or American references to these performances. See

his essay "Raimund und Nestroy in America" in *Österreich und die angelsächsische Welt: Kulturbegegnungen und Vergleiche,* pp. 485 ff.
20. Ibid., p. 488.
21. Otto Rommel, *Die Alt-Wiener Volkskomödie,* p. 929, footnote 16.

Selected Bibliography

Since, at the writing of this book, there exists no up-to-date bibliography on Ferdinand Raimund, every effort was made to render this one as complete and useful as possible. Newspaper articles, manuscripts, and materials of a peripheral nature have been omitted.

PRIMARY SOURCES

1. *Collected and Selected Works* (in chronological order):

Sämtliche Werke, ed. Johann Nepomuk Vogl. 4 vols. 1st ed. Vienna: Rohrmann und Schweigerd, 1837. 2nd ed. Vienna: Karl Hölzl, 1855.

Sämtliche Werke. Nach den Original- und Theatermanuskripten nebst Nachlass und Biographie, eds. Karl Glossy and August Sauer. 3 vols. Vienna: C. Konegen, 1881.

Sämtliche Werke, ed. Eduard Castle. Vienna: Hesses Klassikerausgabe, 1903.

Dramatische Werke, ed. L. Rosner. Leipzig: Knaur, 1905.

Raimunds Werke, ed. Rudolf Fürst. 3 vols. Berlin, Leipzig, Vienna, Stuttgart: Bong and Co., 1909.

Sämtliche Werke, ed. Otto Rommel. 3 vols. Vienna, Teschen, Leipzig: Karl Pruchaska, 1908–1912.

Liebesbriefe, ed. Fritz Brukner. Vienna: Moritz Perles, 1914.

Historisch-kritische Säkularausgabe der Sämtlichen Werke, eds. Fritz Brukner and Eduard Castle, also Franz Hadamowsky and Alfred Orel. 6 vols. Vienna: Anton Schroll, 1924–1934.

Barock: Barocktradition im österreichisch-bayrischen Volkstheater. Deutsche Literatur: Sammlung literarischer Kunst- und Kulturdenkmäler in Entwicklungsreihen, ed. Otto Rommel. Vols. III. and V. Leipzig: Philipp Reclam, 1935–1939.

Dramatische Werke, ed. Gustav Pichler. 2 vols. Vienna: Bergland-Verlag, 1960.

Sämtliche Werke. Nach dem Text der von Fritz Brukner und Eduard Castle besorgten Gesamtausgabe, ed. Friedrich Schreyvogl. Munich: Winkler, 1960.

Das Wiener Volkstheater, ed. Gerhard Helbig. Bremen: Carl Schüne-
mann, 1960. Contains *Der Bauer als Millionär, Der Alpenkönig
und der Menschenfeind,* and *Der Verschwender.*
Gesammelte Werke, ed. Otto Rommel. Vienna: Sigbert Mohn, 1962.
*Der unbekannte Raimund. Gedichte, Tagebuchblätter, Szenen, und
Briefe,* ed. Gutsav Pichler. Vienna: Bergland-Verlag, 1962.
2. *Recent Single Editions:*
Der Barometermacher auf der Zauberinsel, ed. Kurt Benesch. Vienna:
Bergland-Verlag, 1956.
Der Diamant des Geisterkönigs, ed. Gustav Pichler. Vienna: Bergland-
Verlag, 1960.
Der Bauer als Millionär, ed. Ernst Baum. Vienna, Leipzig: Tempsky
and Freytag, 1920.
Der Bauer als Millionär, ed. Otto Rommel. Vienna: Österreichischer
Bundesverlag Hölder, Pichler, Tempsky, 1948.
Der Bauer als Millionär, ed. Kurt Benesch. Vienna: Bergland-Verlag,
1955.
Der Bauer als Millionär, ed. Wilhelm Zentner. Stuttgart: Reclam, 1962.
Die gefesselte Phantasie, ed. Heinz Kindermann. Graz, Vienna:
Stiasny, 1957.
Die gefesselte Phantasie, ed. Gustav Pichler. Vienna: Bergland-Verlag,
1960.
Moisasurs Zauberfluch, ed. Gustav Pichler, adapted by Herbert Johan-
nes Holz. Zurich, Leipzig, Vienna: Amalthea-Verlag, 1958.
Moisasurs Zauberfluch, ed. Gustav Pichler. Vienna: Bergland-Verlag,
1960.
Der Alpenkönig und der Menschenfeind, ed. Gustav Pichler. Vienna:
Bergland-Verlag, 1959.
Der Alpenkönig und der Menschenfeind, ed. Wilhelm Zentner. Stutt-
gart: Reclam, 1959.
Die unheilbringende Krone, ed. Gustav Pichler. Vienna: Bergland-
Verlag, 1959.
Der Verschwender, ed. Otto Rommel. Vienna, Leipzig: Tempsky und
Freytag, 1920.
Der Verschwender, ed. Otto Rommel. Vienna: Österreichischer Bun-
desverlag Hölder, Pichler, Tempsky, 1948.
Der Verschwender, ed. Gustav Pichler. Vienna: Bergland-Verlag, 1958.
Der Verschwender, ed. Wilhelm Zentner. Stuttgart: Reclam, 1963.
3. *English Translations:*
The Spendthrift. Tr. by Erwin Tramer. New York: Frederick Ungar,
1949.
*The Theater of Ferdinand Raimund: The Maid from Fairyland or The
Peasant as Millionaire, Mountain King and Misanthrope.* Tr. by

Selected Bibliography

Corliss Edwin Phillabaum. Unpublished dissertation at Ohio State University, 1962.

SECONDARY SOURCES

Adel, Kurt. *Das Jesuitendrama in Österreich*. Vienna: Bergland-Verlag, 1957.

Alker, Ernst. *Die deutsche Literatur im 19. Jahrhundert*. Stuttgart: Kröner, 1962.

Arnold, Robert Franz. "Ferdinand Raimund in England" in *Beiträge zur neueren Philologie. Festschift für Jakob Schipper*. Vienna, Leipzig: Wilhelm Braumüller, 1902.

————. *Das deutsche Drama*. Munich: C. H. Beck, 1925.

Baechtold-Stäubli, Hans. *Handwörterbuch des deutschen Aberglaubens*. 10 vols. Berlin, Leipzig: Walter de Gruyter & Co., 1927–1942.

Bauer, Anton. *Das Theater in der Josefstadt zu Wien*. Vienna, Munich: Wulf Stratowa, 1957. A history of the *Josefstädter Theater* from its beginnings to 1956, including a list of plays performed.

Bauernfeld, Eduard von. *Wiener Biedermeier. Begegnungen und Erlebnisse*, ed. Karl Jordak. Vienna: Bergland-Verlag, 1960. Contains a chapter entitled "Literarisches Zusammenleben: Grillparzer, Raimund, Anastasius Grün, Nikolaus Lenau," pp. 106–126.

Benda, Oskar. *Die österreichische Kulturidee*. Vienna: Saturn-Verlag, 1936.

Bietak, Wilhelm. "Ferdinand Raimund. Zu seinem 125. Todestag am 5. September, 1961." *Wort in der Zeit*, VII (1961), 54–62.

Blüml, Emil Karl and Gugitz, Gustav. *Alt-Wiener Thespiskarren. Die Frühzeit der Wiener Vorstadtbühnen*. Vienna: Anton Schroll, 1925. Reliable history of travelling theater companies in Austria between 1775 and 1800.

Bolin, Wilhelm. "*Der Menschenfeind*: Eine literarhistorische Studie," *Euphorion*, XIX (1912), 323–334.

Börner, Wilhelm. *Ferdinand Raimund*. Leipzig: Reclam, 1905. Brief and reliable biography.

Brukner, Fritz. *Ferdinand Raimund in der Dichtung seiner Zeitgenossen. Gedichte an Raimund nebst einer Reihe von ungedruckten Briefen*. Vienna: Gilhofer & Ranschburg, 1905. Only a limited edition of 350 copies was printed.

Castelli, Ignaz Franz. *Memoiren meines Lebens*, ed. Josef Bindtner. Munich: G. Müller, 1914.

Castle, Eduard. *Dichter und Dichtung aus Österreich. Ausgewählte Aufsätze*. Vienna: Amandus-Verlag, 1951. Contains chapters on "Die Grundlagen des Volkstheaters," pp. 17–23; "Der Wienerische Hanswurst," pp. 32–41; and "Zur Raimund-Jahrhundertfeier," pp. 51–64.

Castle, Margarethe. "Die Hamburger Katastrophe in Raimunds Leben," *Jahrbuch der Grillparzer-Gesellschaft* (1944), pp. 149–157.

Coar, John Firman. *Studies in German Literature in the Nineteenth Century.* New York: Macmillan, 1903. One of the early treatments of Raimund in American literary criticism.

Cysarz, Herbert. "Raimund und die Metaphysik des Wiener Theaters," in *Welträtsel im Wort.* Vienna: Bergland-Verlag, 1948, pp. 216–245.

Denewa, Wena Stephanowa. *Das österreichische Märchendrama.* Berlin: Otto Elsner, 1940. Treats Raimund as a writer of Biedermeier fairytale dramas.

Dietrich, Margaret. *Europäische Dramaturgie im 19. Jahrhundert.* Graz, Köln, Böhlau, 1961.

Enzinger, Moriz. *Die Entwicklung des Wiener Theaters vom 16. zum 19. Jahrhundert: Stoffe und Motive.* Berlin: Selbstverlag der Gesellschaft für Theatergeschichte, 1918. Considers Raimund as a writer of the Baroque.

Erdmann, Walter. *Ferdinand Raimund: Dichterische Entwicklung, Persönlichkeit, und Lebensschicksal.* Würzburg: Konrad Triltsch, 1943. Informative study of the life and work of Raimund.

Farinelli, Arturo. *Grillparzer und Raimund.* Leipzig: Georg Heinrich Meyer, 1897.

————. "Il poeta dell'anima viennese: Ferdinand Raimund," *Studi germanici,* III (1938), 415, 327–344.

Fechter, Paul. *Das europäische Drama: Geist und Kultur im Spiegel des Theaters.* Vol. I. Mannheim: Bibliographisches Institut, 1956.

Fischer, Ernst. *Von Grillparzer zu Kafka: Essays.* Vienna: Globus-Verlag, 1962.

Flemming, Willi. *Geschichte des Jesuiten-Theaters in den Landen deutscher Zunge.* Berlin: Gesellschaft für Theatergeschichte, 1923.

————. "Die Problematik der Bezeichnung 'Biedermeier,' " *Germanisch-romanische Monatsschrift,* Neue Folge, VIII (1958), 379–388.

Foglar, Adolph. *Grillparzers Ansichten über Literatur, Bühne und Leben.* 2nd ed. Stuttgart: Göschen, 1891.

Fontana, Oskar Maurus. "Die Wiener Grillparzer- Raimund und Nestroy-Neuaufführungen seit 1945," *Maske und Kothurn,* VIII (1963), 132–141.

Frankl, Ludwig August. *Zur Biographie Ferdinand Raimunds.* Vienna, Pest, Leipzig: A. Hartleben, 1884. Unreliable.

Selected Bibliography

————. *Erinnerungen*, ed. Stefan Hock. Prague: Bibliothek deutscher Schriftsteller in Böhmen, 1910.

Fuhrmann, Karl. *Raimunds Kunst und Charakter*. Berlin: Ernst Hofmann und Co., 1913. Attempts to be a supplement to the work on Raimund published by Sauer and Castle.

Glossy, Karl. "Briefe von Ferdinand Raimund an Toni Wagner," *Jahrbuch der Grillparzer-Gesellschaft*, IV (1894), 145–306.

————. "Zur Geschichte der Wiener Theaterzensur," *Jahrbuch der Grillparzer-Gesellschaft*, VII (1897), 238–340.

————. "Ferdinand Raimund" Aus dem Tagebuch des K. K. Hofschauspielers Joseph Schmidt. *Jahrbuch der Grillparzer-Gesellschaft*, VIII (1898), 267–276.

————. "Aus dem Vormärz," *Jahrbuch der Grillparzer-Gesellschaft*, X (1900), 312–347.

————. "Zur Geschichte des Theaters in Wien," *Jahrbuch der Grillparzer-Gesellschaft*, XXV (1915), 1–323.

————. *Kleinere Schriften zu seinem 70. Geburtstag*, ed. by his friends. Vienna, Leipzig: Carl Fromme, 1918. Contains a good bibliography of smaller articles on Raimund, pp. 495–500.

Goedecke, Karl. *Grundriss zur Geschichte der deutschen Dichtung*. 2nd rev. ed. Vol. III. Düsseldorf: L. Ehlermann, 1953.

Gräffer, Franz. *Alt-Wiener Guckkasten*. Vienna: Paul Knepler. n.d.

Gregor, Joseph. *Das Theater in der Josefstadt*. Vienna: Wiener Drucke, 1924. Early historical account of the development of the Josefstädter Theater.

————. *Weltgeschichte des Theaters*. Zurich: Phaidon, 1933.

————. *Das Theater des Volkes in der Ostmark*. Vienna: Deutscher Verlag für Jugend und Volk, 1943.

————. *Das österreichische Theater*. Vienna: Donau-Verlag, 1948.

————. *Der Schauspielführer*. Vol. I. Stuttgart: Hiersemann, 1953.

Greiner, Martin. *Zwischen Biedermeier und Bourgeoisie: Ein Kapitel deutscher Literaturgeschichte*. Göttingen: Vandenhoeck & Ruprecht, 1953. The chapter "Das alte Reich—das alte Österreich," 18–50, treats Raimund and Nestroy.

Gugitz, Gustav. *Der Weiland Kasperl: Johann La Roche, ein Beitrag zur Theater- und Sittengeschichte Alt-Wiens*. Vienna, Prague, Leipzig: E. Strache, 1920.

————. *Die Ehetragödie Ferdinand Raimunds. Nach den unveröffentlichen Akten des Wiener Stadtgerichtes im Archiv der Stadt Wien*. Vienna: Wiener Bibliophile Gesellschaft, 1956. This limited edition of 220 copies deals with Luise Raimund's extramarital lovelife.

Hadamowsky, Franz. *Das Theater in der Leopoldstadt. 1781–1860.*

*Kataloge der Theatersammlung der Nationalbibliothek in Wien,
Vol. III.* Vienna: Generaldirektion der Nationalbibliothek, 1934.
————. Die Commedia dell'Arte in Österreich und ihre Wirkung auf
das Wiener Volkstheater," *Maske und Kothurn,* III (1957), 312–
316.

Hermand, Jost. *Die literarische Formenwelt des Biedermeiers.* Giessen:
Wilhelm Schmitz, 1958.

Herterich, Franz. *Das Burgtheater und seine Sendung.* Vienna: Paul
Neff, 1948.

Hinck, Walter. *Das deutsche Lustspiel des 17. und 18. Jahrhunderts
und die italienische Komödie.* Stuttgart: J. B. Metzler, 1965.

Hock, Stefan. "Von Raimund bis Anzengruber," *Jahrbuch der Grillparzer-Gesellschaft,* XV (1905), 31–60.

Hofmannsthal, Hugo von. "Ferdinand Raimund," *Einleitung zu einer
Sammlung seiner Lebensdokumente. Prosa* III (Frankfurt a. M.:
S. Fischer, 1952), pp. 471–478.

Holl, Karl. *Geschichte des deutschen Lustspiels.* Leipzig: J. J. Weber,
1923. Treats Raimund as a Romantic author.

Höllerer, Walter. *Zwischen Klassik und Moderne: Lachen und Weinen
in der Dichtung einer Übergangszeit.* Stuttgart: Ernst Klett, 1958.

Kahl, Kurt. *Raimund.* Velber: Friedrich, 1967.

Kann, Robert A. *A Study in Austrian Intellectual History: From Late
Baroque to Romanticism.* New York: Frederick A. Praeger, 1960.

Katann, Oskar. *Gesetz im Wandel.* Munich, Vienna, Innsbruck: Tyro-
lia-Verlag, 1932. Contains a useful study of Riamund's *Der Bauer
als Millionär,* pp. 26–50.

Kilian, Eugen. "Raimunds *Gefesselte Phantasie,*" *Jahrbuch der Grillparzer-Gesellschaft,* XII (1902), 191–198.

Kindermann, Heinz. "Shakespeare und das deutsche Volkstheater,"
Jahrbuch der Grillparzer-Gesellschaft, XLIII (1933).

————. "Die Commedia dell'Arte und das deutsche Volkstheater."
Leipzig: Heinrich Keller, 1938.

————. *Ferdinand Raimund: Lebenswerk und Wirkungsraum eines
deutschen Volksdramatikers.* Vienna, Leipzig: Adolf Luser, 1940.
Informative and perceptive study of the life and work of Raimund.

————. *Theatergeschichte Europas. Vol. V. Aufklärung-Romantik.*
Salzburg: Otto Müller, 1962.

Kluckhohn, Paul. "Biedermeier als literarische Epochenbezeichnung,"
*Deutsche Vierteljahrsschrift für Literaturwissenschaft und Geis-
tesgeschichte,* XIII (1935), 1–43.

Knudsen, Hans. *Deutsche Theatergeschichte.* Stuttgart: Alfred Kröner,
1959.

Kober, Margarete. *Das deutsche Märchendrama.* Frankfurt a. M.:
Moritz Diesterweg, 1925.

Selected Bibliography

Koch, Franz. *Idee und Wirklichkeit: Deutsche Dichtung zwischen Romantik und Naturalismus*. Düsseldorf: Louis Ehlermann, 1956. Contains a useful study of "Raimund und Nestroy," II, 164–192.

Körner, Josef. *Bibliographisches Handbuch des deutschen Schrifttums*. Bern: A. Francke, 1949.

Kosch, Wilhelm. *Deutsches Literaturlexikon*. Bern: A. Francke, (n.d.) III, 2152–2153.

Kulturamt der Stadt Wien, ed. *Die Raimundfeier der Stadt Wien*. Vienna, Leipzig: Deutscher Verlag für Jugend und Volk, 1940. Contains a poetic prologue by Josef Weinheber and articles by Josef Gregor, Hanns Blaschke, Rainer Schlösser, and Heinz Kindermann.

Kutscher, Arthur. *Das Salzburg Barocktheater*. Vienna, Leipzig, Munich: Rikola, 1924.

Leitich, Ann Tizia. *Wiener Biedermeier: Kultur, Kunst und Leben der alten Kaiserstadt vom Wiener Kongress bis zum Sturmjahr 1848*. Bielefeld, Leipzig: Velhagen & Klasing, 1941. Contains a well-illustrated chapter on "Theater und Theaterleut," pp. 168–183.

Mann, Otto. *Geschichte des deutschen Dramas*. Stuttgart: Alfred Kröner, 1963.

Meyer, Richard M. *Deutsche Literatur des 19. Jahrhunderts*. Berlin: Georg Bondi, 1900.

Möller, Alfred. *Ferdinand Raimund: Bilder von seinem Lebensweg*. Graz: Ulrich Moser, 1923.

Mülher, Robert. "Raimond und der Humor," *Zeitschrift für deutsche Philologie*, LXIV (1939), 257–268.

Müller, Hans von. *Zehn Generationen deutscher Dichter und Denker*. Berlin: Frankfurter Verlagsanstalt, 1928.

Müller-Guttenbrunn, Adam. *Im Jahrhundert Grillparzers: Literatur und Lebensbilder aus Österreich*. Leipzig: Georg Heinrich Meyer, 1895.

Nadler, Josef. *Literaturgeschichte Österreichs*. 2nd ed. Salzburg: Otto Müller, 1951.

Nagl, Johann Willibald and Zeidler, Jakob, also Eduard Castle. *Deutsch-Österreichische Literaturgeschichte*. 4 vols. Vienna: C. Fromme, 1899–1937. Sees Raimund as a product of the Baroque.

Nash, Martin A. "*Die gefesselte Phantasie* and Ferdinand Raimund," *The German Quarterly*, XXXVI (1963), 14–24.

Niederführ, Hans. *Alt-Wiener Theater*. Vienna, Berlin: Karl H. Bischoff, 1942.

Perry, Henry Ten Eyck. *Masters of Dramatic Comedy and Their Social Themes*. Cambridge: Harvard University Press, 1939.

Petermann, Reinhard E. *Wien von Jahrhundert zu Jahrhundert.* Vienna, Leipzig, New York: Gerlach & Wiedling, 1927.

Pichler, Gustav, ed., *Raimund Almanach.* Vienna, Innsbruck, Wiesbaden: Rudolf M. Rohrer, 1956.

――――. "Ferdinand Raimund" in *Neue Österreichische Biographie* (Vienna, 1957), X, 9–16.

――――, ed., *Raimund Almanach.* Vienna: Bergland-Verlag, 1959.

――――, ed., *Raimund Almanach.* Vienna: Bergland-Verlag, 1963.

Politzer, Heinz. "Ferdinand Raimunds *Menschenfeind,*" in *Neue Rundschau,* LXVI (1955), 110–124; also in *Das deutsche Drama,* ed. Benno von Wiese. (Düsseldorf: August Bagel, 1958), II, 9–22.

――――. "Alt-Weiner Theaterlieder," *Forum,* VIII (1961), 26–29.

Pollak, Gustav. *Franz Grillparzer and the Austrian Drama.* New York: Dodd, Mead and Co., 1907.

Prisching, Rudolf. "Raimunds Anfänge." Eine Studie. Program des K. K. Kaiser-Franz-Josef-Staatsgymnasiums in Mährisch-Ostrau für das Schuljahr 1901 / 1902.

――――. "*Der Verschwender.*" Eine Studie. Program des K. K. Kaiser-Franz-Josef-Staatsgymnasiums in Mährich-Ostrau für das Schuljahr 1910 / 1911.

――――. "Raimunds Mädchen aus der Feenwelt" in *Alt-Wiener Kalender* (Zurich, Leipzig, Vienna: Amalthea-Verlag, 1926), pp. 90–114.

Rauscher, Otto. *Raimunds Leben in Bildern.* Leipzig: Bibliographisches Institut, 1936. Treats Raimund as a Biedermeier playwright; also contains forty-seven photographs pertaining to his life and work.

Reboul, J. *Un grand précurseur des Romantiques, Raimund.* Nizza, 1912.

Reischl, Friedrich. *Wien zur Biedermeierzeit. Volksleben in Wiens Vorstädten nach zeitgenössischen Schilderungen.* Vienna: Gerlach & Wiedling, 1921. Covers Vienna's cultural activities between 1800 and 1850.

Rieder, Heinz. *Wiener Vormärz: Das Theater, das literarische Leben, die Zensur.* Vienna: Bergland-Verlag, 1959.

Röbbeling, Hermann. "Raimund und das Burgtheater," *Jahrbuch der Grillparzer-Gesellschaft,* XXXIV (1937), 66–78.

Rommel, Otto. *Ein Jahrhundert Alt-Wiener Parodien.* Vienna, Leipzig: Österreichischer Bundesverlag, 1930.

――――. "Der Wienerische Hanswurst als Dramatiker," *Jahrbuch der Gesellschaft für Wiener Theaterforschung,* I (1944), 129 ff.

――――. *Die grossen Figuren der Alt-Wiener Volkskomödie.* Vienna: Bindenschild, 1946.

Selected Bibliography

―――. *Ferdinand Raimund und die Vollendung des Alt-Wiener Zauberstückes.* Vienna: Bindenschild, 1947.

―――. *Die Alt-Wiener Volkskomödie: Ihre Geschichte vom barocken Welttheater bis zum Tod Nestroys.* Vienna: Anton Schroll, 1952. A comprehensive history of the Old Viennese Popular Theater.

―――. "The Old Viennese Folk Theatre," *World Theatre,* X (1961), 2, 121–128.

―――. "Johann Nestroy: Der Satiriker auf der Altwiener Komödien-bühne" in *Johann Nestroy. Gesammelte Werke.* (Vienna: Anton Schroll, 1948–1949), I, 9–189.

Rosenthal, Friedrich. "Wieland und Österreich," *Jahrbuch der Grill-parzer-Gesellschaft,* XXIV (1913), 55–102.

―――. *Die Wanderbühne: Ein Beitrag zur Not, Rettung und Gene-sung des deutschen Theaters.* Vienna, Leipzig: Amalthea-Verlag, 1922.

―――. *Theater in Österreich.* Vienna, Leipzig: A. Hartleben, 1926.

Sauer, August. "Ferdinand Raimund" in *Allgemeine deutsche Bio-graphie* (Leipzig: Duncker & Humblot, 1888), XXVII, 736–755.

―――. *Gesammelte Reden und Aufsätze zur Geschichte der Literatur in Österreich und Deutschland.* Vienna, Leipzig: Carl Fromme, 1903. Contains a useful chapter "Ferdinand Raimund: Eine Char-akteristik," pp. 240–274.

Scheyer, Ernst. "Biedermeier in der Literatur- und Kunstgeschichte," *Aurora,* XX, 13–19.

Schmidt, Adalbert. *Dichtung und Dichter Österreichs im 19. und 20. Jahrhundert.* Vol. I. Salzburg, Stuttgart: Bergland-Verlag, 1964.

Schmidt, Erich. *Charakteristiken.* 2nd ed. Berlin: Weidmann, 1902. See pp. 363–383.

Schmidt, Leopold. "Hanswurst und verwandte Gestalten," *Jahrbuch für Wiener Theaterforschung,* II (1946).

―――. *Das deutsche Volksschauspiel: Ein Handbuch.* Berlin: Erich Schmidt, 1962.

Schüssel, Therese. *Kultur des Barock in Österreich.* Graz: Stiasny, 1960.

Seidl, Johann Gabriel. *Wiens Umgebungen: Nach eigenen Wanderun-gen und mit Benützung der besten und neuesten Quellen ge-schildert.* Vienna: Mörschner & Jasper, 1826.

Seyfried, Ferdinand von. *Rückschau in das Theaterleben Wiens seit den letzten fünfzig Jahren.* Vienna: Selbstverlag des Verfassers, 1864.

Smekal, Richard, ed. *Ferdinand Raimunds Lebensdokumente.* Vienna, Berlin: Wiener Literarische Anstalt, 1920.

―――. *Grillparzer und Raimund. Funde und Studien.* Vienna, Leipzig: Barth, 1920.

Sprengler, Josef. "Ferdinand Raimund," *Hochland,* XXXV (1937 / 1938), 371–380.

Stigler-Fuchs, Margarethe von. *Wiener Theater vor und hinter den Kulissen.* Vienna: Wilhelm Andermann, 1943.

Stoessl, Otto. *Geist und Gehalt.* Vienna: Saturn-Verlag, 1935.

Straubinger, O. Paul. "The Reception of Raimund and Nestroy in England and America" in *Österreich und die angelsächsische Welt: Kulturbegegnungen und Vergleiche,* ed. Otto Hietsch (Vienna, Stuttgart: Wilhelm Braumüller, 1961) pp. 481–494.

Taylor, Alan John P. *The Habsburg Monarchy, 1809–1918.* London: Hamish Hamilton, 1948.

Thurn, Rudolf Payer von, ed. *Wiener Haupt- und Staatsaktionen.* 2 vols. Vienna: Verlag des literarischen Vereins, 1908–1910.

Trojan, Felix. *Theater an der Wien: Schauspieler und Volksstücke in den Jahren 1850–1875.* Vienna, Leipzig: Wila, 1923.

Trutter, Hans. "Neue Forschungen über Stranitzky und seine Werke," *Euphorion,* XXIV (1922), 28–60.

Tschulik, Werner. *Die österreichische Dichtung im Rahmen der Weltliteratur.* 7th ed. Vienna: Österreichischer Bundesverlag Hölder, Pichler, Tempsky, 1963.

Tyrolt, Rudolph. *Ferdinand Raimund.* Vienna, 1892.

―――. *Allerlei von Theater und Kunst.* Vienna, Leipzig: Wilhelm Braumüller, 1909.

Ullmayer, Franz. *Memoiren des patriotischen Volks- und Theater Dichters Carl Meisl.* Vienna: Jakob Dirnböck, 1868.

Vancsa, Kurt. *Ferdinand Raimund: Ein Dichter des Biedermeier.* Innsbruck, Vienna: Tryolia-Verlag, 1936.

Vincenti, L. "Comico e dramatico nelle fiabe di Ferdinand Raimund" in *Saggi di letterature tedesca.* Milan, Naples, 1953. See pp. 131–184.

Vogelsang, Hans. "Ferdinand Raimund: Ideal und Wirklichkeit," *Österreich in Geschichte und Literatur,* IX (1965), 264–278.

Waniek, Herbert. *Die Lieder Ferdinand Raimunds. Mit einer Chronik in Daten und Zitaten.* Vienna: Universal-Verlag, 1940.

Weidmann, Franz Carl. *Die Umgebungen Wiens.* Vienna: Carl Armbruster, 1823.

Weigel, Hans. *Flucht vor der Grösse: Beiträge zur Erkenntnis und Selbsterkenntnis Österreichs.* Vienna: Wollzeilen-Verlag, 1960.

Wertheimer, Paul, ed. *Alt-Wiener Theater. Schilderungen von Zeitgenossen.* Vienna: Paul Knepler, 1920.

Wolzogen, Hans von. *Ferdinand Raimund. Eine Erinnerung und eine*

Selected Bibliography

Mahnung. Berlin: Selbstverlag, 1906. Traces Raimund's influence upon the work of Richard Wagner.

Wurzbach, Constant von. "Ferdinand Raimund" in *Biographisches Lexikon des Kaisertums Österreich,* (Vienna: Verlag der K. K. Hof- und Staatsdruckerei, 1872.) XXIII, 254–278.

Zausmer, Otto. *Lebendes, schaffendes Biedermeier.* Vienna: Wiener Urania, 1936.

———, ed., *Raimund Almanach.* Vienna, Innsbruck: Tyrolia, 1936.

APPENDIX

1. *Dissertations:* (unpublished)

Arndt, K. S. N. "Ferdinand Raimund: An Appraisal of the Serious Elements in His Plays," Connecticut, 1966.

Bennett, E. "The Supernatural in German Drama of the Early Nineteenth Century," Birmingham, 1919.

Berkhout, A. P. "Biedermeier und poetischer Realismus," Amsterdam, 1942.

Bittner, L. "Ensemble um Raimund im *Leopoldstädter Theater,*" Vienna, 1948.

Bramahs-Umek, H. "Die Kunst der Metapher bei Ferdinand Raimund," Vienna, 1936.

Brody, A. "Die Elemente des Stegreiftheaters bei Raimund," Vienna, 1953.

deLaporte, E. "Studien über die Beziehung Ferdinand Raimunds zur Romantik," Kiel, 1953.

Ebel, B. E. "The Expression of the Comic in the Plays of Ferdinand Raimund," Stanford, 1956.

Futter, E. "Raimunds schauspielerische Partnerinnen," Vienna, 1966.

Grilk, W. H. "Ferdinand Raimund as a Character in Fictional Writing between 1854 and 1946," University of Michigan (in progress).

Gürster, E. "Ferdinand Raimund und das Theater," Munich, 1920.

Haimerl, J. "Ferdinand Raimund, seine Vorgänger und seine Zeitgenossen," Vienna, 1912.

Hashagen, E. "Der Beruf des Dichters in den Anschauungen der Biedermeierzeit," Tübingen, 1938.

Hoefele, E. "Monolog und Theaterlied bei Raimund und Nestroy," Freiburg im Breisgau (in progress).

James, D. "The Reflection of Viennese Life and Society in the Dramas of Ferdinand Raimund," London, 1964.

Kert, L. "Raimund und Nestroy, zwei Wiener Volksschauspieler," Vienna, 1936.

Koch, Curt. "Grillparzers *Ahnfrau* und die Wiener Volksdramatik," Leipzig, 1911.

Krone, W. "Wenzel Müller: Ein Beitrag zur Geschichte der komischen Oper," Berlin, 1906.

Kubasta, H. "Die Bildung der Raimundlegende," Vienna, 1937.

Lamel, A. "Das Tanzspiel in Raimunds Dramen," Vienna, 1940.

Lobeck, H. "Subjektivismus und Objektivismus in Romantik und Biedermeier," Bonn, 1948.

Lutter, S. M. "Das Barocktheater und sein Einfluss auf Ferdinand Raimund," Vienna, 1934.

Merck, Grete. "Raimunds *Verschwender:* Wesen und Werk eines Romantikers," Marburg, 1925 (published in 1927).

Meyer, W. "Werden und Wesen des Wiener Hanswurst," Leipzig, 1931.

Moss, W. E. "Traditional Elements in the Plays of Raimund," Kings College, London, 1954.

Nagy, Alexander. "Raimunds ungarische Beziehungen," Budapest, 1920.

Olles, H. "Zerissenheit bei Raimund und Nestroy," Frankfurt a. M., 1954.

Phillabaum, E. C. "The Theater of Ferdinand Raimund," Ohio State, 1962.

Rehm, H. "Die Entstehung des Wiener Volkstheaters im Anfang des 18. Jahrhunderts," Munich, 1936.

Schaumann, F. "Gestalt und Funktion des Mythos in Raimunds Bühnenwerken," Berlin (in progress).

Wondrusch, E. "Ferdinand Raimunds Schaffen im Spiegel der Wiener Presse," Vienna, 1947.

Zeeh, K. "Die Wiener Mundart bei Ferdinand Raimund," Vienna, 1964.

Zehl, E. "Märchenmotive in Raimunds Zauberspielen," Vienna, 1944.

2. *Fictional treatment of the life and work of Raimund:*

Aichinger, Gerhard. *Hochzuverehrendes Publikum.* Leipzig: Der junge Bühnenvertrieb, 1942. (drama)

Bäuerle, Adolf. *Therese Krones.* Vienna: Jaspers Witwe Hügel, 1854. (novel)

——. *Ferdinand Raimund.* Vienna: Eduard Hügel, 1855. (novel)

Berla, A. *Die Komiker Wiens* in *Novellenzeitung,* June, 1858–April, 1859. (novel)

Danszky, Eduard Paul. *Da leg' ich meinen Hobel hin.* Berlin: Zsolnay, 1939. (novel)

Eigl, Kurt. *Volksschauspiel vom armen Ferdinand Raimund.* Vienna, 1939. (drama)

Elmar-Swiedak, Karl. *Ferdinand Raimund. Künstlerkizze mit Gesang in drei Akten.* Vienna: J. B. Wallishausser, 1851. (drama)

Selected Bibliography

Hirschfeld, Lisl. *Gegen den Strom.* Last scene of Act IV in *Raimund-Almanach,* (Vienna, Innsbruck, Wiesbaden: Rudolf M. Rohrer, 1956), pp. 87–90. (drama)

Hollander-Lossow, Else. *Hinter der lachenden Maske.* Hannover: Sponholtz, 1939. (novel)

Hrastnik, Franz. "Zwei Szenen aus dem Schauspiel *Die Verschwenderin,*" in *Raimund-Almanach,* ed. Gustav Pichler (Vienna: Bergland-Verlag, 1959), pp. 54–59. (drama)

Jacob, H. E. *Der gefesselte Raimund* in *Dämonen und Narren.* Frankfurt a. M.: Rütten & Löning, 1927. (short story)

Jantsch, Heinrich and Calliano, Alexander. *Ferdinand Raimund: Ein Gemälde aus der Coulissenwelt.* Leipzig: Reclam, 1892. (drama)

Karlweis, Carl. *In Gutenstein. Genrebild in einem Akt* in *Raimund-Almanach,* ed. Gustav Pichler (Vienna, Innsbruck, Wiesbaden: Rudolf M. Rohrer, 1956), pp. 65–80. (drama)

Koselka, Fritz. *Zum goldenen Halbmond.* Munich, 1935, unpublished. (operetta by Robert Stolz)

Mell, Max. *Raimunds Gedicht: Das Donauweibchen.* Leipzig: Insel-Verlag, 1937. (poem)

Pauli, Herta. *Toni.* Vienna: Zsolnay, 1935. (novel)

Prossinag, Ernst. *Der Komödiant.* Vienna, 1925. (drama)

Reuper, Julius. *Ferdinand Raimund.* Dresden: Meinhold, 1869. (drama)

Rismondo, Piero. "Szene aus *Raimund: Ein Wiener Mysterium*" in *Raimund-Almanach,* ed. Gustav Pichler (Vienna: Bergland-Verlag, 1963), pp. 107–111. (drama.)

Schuck, Pankraz. *Raimunds letzte Liebe.* Leipzig: Hesse & Becker, 1914. (novel)

———. *Rappelkopf.* 1940. (short story)

Stössl, Otto. *Raimunds Wiederkehr.* 1936, unpublished. (Festspiel)

Strobl, Karl Hans. *Ein Schicksalstag Ferdinand Raimunds.* Vienna, Leipzig: Adolf Luser, 1940. (short story)

Stüber, Fritz Gunther. *Rappelkopf.* Vienna: Wiener Literarische Anstalt, 1922. (novel)

Weidmann, Franz Karl. *Dem Andenken Raimunds, oder die Grenze der Vergänglichkeit* in *Ferdinand Raimund in der Dichtung seiner Zeitgenossen,* ed. Fritz Brukner (Vienna: Gilhofer & Ranschburg, 1905), pp. 47–63. (drama)

Wüst, Leni. *Der Zauberer von Wien.* Leipzig: A. H. Payne, 1938. (novel)

Index

Index

Index

Wawra, Hermann, 59
Weh' dem der lügt, 47
Werthers, Leiden, 38
Weiskern, Friedrich Wilhelm, 29
Weiss, Eduard, 59
Weissvogels Witwenstand, 52
Werthes, Clemens August, 21
Wieland, Christoph Martin, 61
"Wiener Theaterzeitung", 38, 50
"Wiener Zeitschrift", 52
Wilhelm Tell, 45

Wimmer, Fritz, 37
Wurstio, Johanno, 30

Yates, Frederick, 91
Yates, Henry, 92
Ydor, der Wanderer, 45

Zauberflöte, 32
Zauberstück, 36
Zeno, Apostolo, 23